JOHN WILKINS.

THE
AUTOBIOGRAPHY
OF AN
ENGLISH GAMEKEEPER

(JOHN WILKINS, OF STANSTEAD, ESSEX)

EDITED BY

ARTHUR H. BYNG AND STEPHEN M. STEPHENS

ILLUSTRATED

SECOND AND REVISED EDITION

London

T FISHER UNWIN

PATERNOSTER SQUARE

1892

CONTENTS.

BOOK I.

CHAP.		PAGE
I.	Early recollections	9
II.	My first affray with poachers	21
III.	Concerning trapping, snaring and other matters	35
IV.	Catching my first poacher	50
V.	What was it?	62
VI.	Harry Wright's sandy rabbit	70
VII.	The end of Poacher Bob	76
VIII.	Dabber Harding and Old Sarah	85
IX.	Concerning Dick and other things	93
X.	Dick's Ghost	98
XI.	Harry Wright caught in a trap	104
XII.	The money coiners	118
XIII.	Of Alexander	131

BOOK II.

CHAP.		PAGE
I.	Concerning dogs	151
II.	Inasmuch as to retrievers	171
III.	Inasmore as to retrievers	178
IV.	Inasmost as to retrievers	190
V.	How I got my last job	193
VI.	Concerning game and things	196
VII.	Mine host and friend Baldwin	203
VIII.	Hares, rabbits and farmers	212
IX.	Poachers' dogs, and how to kill them	222
X.	A bloody fray	229
XI.	The sequel to the fray — Joslin's donkey	242
XII.	Haggy Player caught and lost	250
XIII.	Joslin as a witness — Duckey Phillips	256
XIV.	Duckey's father—his death	264
XV.	Cubs, foxes and vixens	270
XVI.	Snaring and trapping foxes	284

CONTENTS.

BOOK III.

CHAP.	PAGE
I.—Shooting extraordinary	297
II.—The Major, the Parson and Humphries	306
III.—Encore Humphries	316
IV.—The slaughter of vermin	325
V.—More poachers and poaching	336
VI.—Monk's conversion	345
VII.—Encore Monk	351
VIII.—Poaching again	356
IX.—Chiefly canine	371
X.—Of rabbits	378
XI.—Chats about pheasants	383
XII.—Ferrets and rabbits	392
XIII.—Discursive and academic	400
XIV.—Ferrets and rabbits again	403
XV.—Night watching	411
XVI.—Humphries reappears	418
XVII.—Humphries reappears and disappears	425

LIST OF ILLUSTRATIONS.

John Wilkins	Frontispiece
The identification of "Coughtrey, the poacher," by the villagers	Facing p. 80
Wilkins smashing the rotten eggs in Harry Wright's pocket	Facing p. 113
Wilkins and the policeman chasing the coiners	Facing p. 119
Dog breaking: Wilkins speaking seriously to the dog	Facing p. 156
Jones stopping the other poachers from killing Wilkins	Facing p. 240

PREFACE.

THE Editors of this book make no apology for presenting it to the public. Until now the Gamekeepers of England have kept their experiences to themselves, or have merely dispensed them, in fragmentary fashion, to the village Corydon or the rural Amaryllis. Reminiscences of the hunting field, the turf, the pulpit, the bar, and the stage have appeared in profusion, but John Wilkins is the first of his profession to publish genuine reminiscences.

After no little consideration, it has been decided to insert the real names of the individuals mentioned in the following pages, with the exception of Major Symons and Jones, the ex-keeper, who are fictitious in name though real in character. Most of them are now dead, but, be they living or dead, the Editors claim that concerning them, nothing is extenuate or aught set down in malice.

PREFACE.

Finally, our share of the work has been small. Assuming that Mr. Wilkins' stage name is Esau, and that our stage name is Jacob, the words are for the most part the words of Esau, and the writing is the writing of Jacob. We feel that nothing further is wanting to the extreme lucidity of this explanation.

Our thanks are due to Mr. Sidney Starr, for his labour in illustrating the present Autobiography.

ARTHUR H. BYNG.
STEPHEN M. STEPHENS.

BOOK I.

CHAPTER I.

EARLY RECOLLECTIONS.

I REMEMBER, sixty-three years ago, my father, Luke Wilkins, was gamekeeper for Mr. Key, of Tring Park, Herts. Mr. Yates lived at Tring Park before Mr. Key, and Sir Drummond Smith before Mr. Yates. My father was gamekeeper to all three, in succession. I remember seeing Mr. Key "chaired,"—that is, carried round the town in a chair, my father and others following and firing off their guns.

I remember, too, that at that time we lived

in the "Summer House," a cottage set in the wood near the Park. My father subsequently obtained the situation of head gamekeeper to Lord Lake, so we left the Summer House, and went to live at Dunnell's Hole, a few miles from Tring.

We left Lord Lake's about the year 1823,* and went to Boxmoor. My father was, for a long time, unable to obtain a situation as gamekeeper, so he did odd jobs, such as helping in the stables at Westbrook House Boxmoor, and working in the brick-yard at Tring. At last, in the year 1825, he obtained a situation as gamekeeper to Mr. John Fuller, of German House, Chesham, Bucks. Here my father lived for thirty years, at the end of which time he died, and was buried at Hyde Heath Chapel. When Mr. John Fuller died, Mr. Benjamin Fuller came to German House, and he kept on my father as gamekeeper. Mr. Benjamin Fuller is—or rather was, for

* These reminiscences were first written some few years ago.—EDITORS.

he is now dead—the father of Mr. Stratton Fuller who at present lives at German House.

I remember my father well. A most resolute and determined man he was—a first-rate keeper, and an excellent dog trainer. He had a very hasty and violent temper, but notwithstanding this, he was a strictly honest man, and taught me to be upright and truthful in all my dealings, which teaching I have always endeavoured to follow.

When I was nine years old, I attended the British School, at Chesham: and one day I saw four or five men go into the village shop, and buy some brass wire. I guessed what they wanted it for, though they little thought that a pair of sharp eyes were watching their movements. The men came out of the shop, and went off by Mr. Fuller's place, up the Weedon Hill Road, towards Monk's Wood. I at once informed Mr. Fuller of what I had seen. He then sent me to tell my father; but father was not at home, so I started off for Monk's Wood alone. It was about four o'clock in the afternoon, in the month of November. I reached the footpath under Monk's Wood, and there I met the purchasers of the brass wire. They shouted to me:—

"Hullo, young feller, where are you off to? We've lost our donkeys; have you seen 'em about anywhere?"

"Yes," said I. "I see some now." Which was my idea of humour, in those days.

Then they muttered together, and one of them laughed.

"Look here, youngster," said one man, gruffly, "We've lost our donkeys and ourselves, too."

I walked on rapidly for a few paces, and then, turning round, shouted back at them:—"I don't believe you're lost, or your donkeys, either." And, thereupon, I dived round the elbow of the wood into a road leading out of the footpath amongst the trees, thinking it quite time to give leg-bail.

I had not proceeded far before a heavy hand was laid on my shoulder; I was about to cry out when I heard a whisper:—"All right, Jack," and turning, I confronted my father, who, I soon learnt, had been watching the men all along. I told him what I had seen and done and he commended me for my sharpness. I relate this because it made me take a liking for keepering.

A few months afterwards I left the British School and was put to look after the pheasants during the breeding season, and this I continued to do for some few years. I used to keep my watch in an old tilted cart, armed with a light single-barrelled gun belonging to my father, and having, for company, a poor, worn-out retriever dog. One day, I saw a hawk pounce down on one of the young pheasants, taking it up in his talons, and flying away with it. I raised my gun, and fired; the hawk dropped to the ground, dead, but still gripping its prey. Wonderful to relate the pheasant was unhurt, and immediately ran off to the coop, to its mother. Mr. John Fuller had the hawk stuffed, and it can be seen, to this day, at German House, where Mr. Stratton Fuller now resides; the people there, moreover, will tell you the same tale as I have told about it.

Just before the shooting, and whilst I was still at school, my father, as a great treat, allowed me to walk through the woods with him one Saturday, that day being a holiday. We went through Monk's Wood, and, at the end of the wood, my father sat down on the stump of a tree, for about twenty minutes, to see if any poachers were coming from Weedon Hill Road or Coppysons Lane; this was a very quiet part, and a favorite way with poachers. Having sat awhile, and finished his pipe, he knocked out the ashes, and then instructed me as follows; I listening with close attention.

"John, you sit here till I come back. I'm going round Beech Wood, Odd's, and Bois Wood. If you happen to see any of those chaps after my hares, don't you be afraid; just go straight at them, and sing out, ' Here they are, father, here they are! Look out, father, they're coming towards you;' stand still and they'll run straight into your arms!"

All this was accompanied with pantomimic gestures, my father striking attitudes of a fearful and wonderful kind, in his anxiety to impress upon me the way the thing really ought to be done. "They don't know who's about, you see," he went on. "And, if you show yourself, and make a row, they're sure to bolt; what we want is to prevent them taking our hares."

"Very good, father," said I; and so he turned on his heel and left me, and very proud of my job I was, too.

I kept a sharp look out, eyes and ears on the alert, but there was nothing moving until dark; then, owing I suppose to the strain on my nerves, I fancied I heard a rustle, and started up, but, to my great disappointment, my poachers turned out to be a hare or a rabbit. So I sat on for a long time, until I began to wonder what had become of father; could he have got a job on in some other wood, or had he forgotten me altogether? It appeared, subsequently, that the latter was the case.

Father reached home, and put on his list slippers; lit his pipe, and settled himself comfortably in a chair, when my mother asked what had become of the boy.

"What! ain't he home yet?" asked father, laconically.

"No; where did you leave him?" "At the Chalk Pit."

"When?" "Soon after dinner."

"What for?" "To look out for poachers. I told him to sit there 'till I came back, and now I've clean forgot all about him."

"Then p'raps he's sitting there, now."

"Very like." And then father and mother had a few words, with the result that father sent off Jim Keen to look after me. Of Jim I shall speak later on, and, at present, I may mention that he was born at Little Missenden, Bucks, and was now under keeper to Mr. Fuller. Father gave Jim very particular orders about me. "You will find the boy close to the Chalk Pit; don't call him 'till you get quite close, or he may fall into the pit, and break every bone in his body." This pit was a very deep one, and I've seen my father stand at the top, and shoot a rabbit in the bottom, when it was odds on the rabbit as against the gun.

It was after eleven at night, and I was still on the watch, when I thought I heard some one on the move, and sprang to my feet, ready for a call:—"Look out, father, here they are." Then, to my surprise and disappointment, I heard a voice shout:—

"Stand still, John; don't stir a peg till I come to you." It was Jim's voice.

"All right, Jim," I replied, and he came and took my hand, and led me into the Half-Way-House Lane. There was no moon, so it was pitch dark; he went up the Lane to Hyde Heath, and I down, half a mile to home.

When I reached our house, my parents asked me if I did not feel frightened, "No," said I, "But I felt a bit hungry." And with that I turned to at my supper, and so, afterwards, to "allie couchay." *

One day I was all alone, up in White's Wood, minding the tame birds, when a fearful thunderstorm came on. I crept into the tilted cart, which I sometimes used to sleep in when minding the birds at night; my dog curled up underneath, and thus, with my gun beside me, comfortably in the dry, I took no notice of the

* This in the original manuscript. Presumably meaning—allez coucher—EDITORS.

weather. After the storm, father came and took me home with him, and then he and mother talked very seriously about it; they said the thunder and lightning was simply awful.

"Where you not afraid, John?" asked my father.

"No," said I, shortly. I was only eleven years old then, but I can seem to see my father and mother, now, as they looked at me in astonishment, amazed at my answer, and its evident sincerity.

"And why were you not afraid?" they asked.

"I thought that the Lord was trying to frighten me, and I determined that I would not be frightened," said I, simply. I could not say such a thing, now, but, although my answer appears irreverent, it was more the outcome of childish heedlessness than any spirit of bravado, for I have always acknowledged the Almighty power and will of our Heavenly Father. I do not wish to boast, or draw the long bow, in describing the events of my life; and, indeed, there are many gentlemen still living who can testify as to the absolute truth of everything I relate in this book. As a boy and man I was wholly devoid of fear in all matters relating to my vocation; as shooting, trapping, watching, and catching poachers: the excitement of my work seemed to leave no room for fear, and I would handle the most savage dog, or the most dangerous poacher, without a moment's hesitation. But I don't like horses; I am not at home with them, and I would sooner walk ten miles than get on a horse's back. With anything else I am all right directly I get to close quarters; what would unnerve most men just brings me up to the scratch. For instance, with a lion or tiger, I should feel nervous whilst it was some way off, but, when I got close, I should think of nothing but killing him; the possibility of his killing me would not enter into my calculations at all. The same with poachers. On a dark night, in a lonely wood, looking forward to an encounter with desperate men, many of the bravest of us are nervous; but such a situation, somehow, always brings my courage up to the sticking point. I have known, too, some watchers, whom nothing would induce to go near certain woods at night, for fear of ghosts; even poachers are affected that way, sometimes. Although, however, I have seen some remarkably curious things happen, as I will relate presently, I was never afraid of ghosts.

CHAPTER II.

MY FIRST AFFRAY WITH POACHERS.

WHEN I was a lad of thirteen, my first serious encounter with poachers occurred. Father had received warning that three or four poachers were coming, one night, to steal some tame pheasants that were in the meadow, close by our house. I had seen five men go up from Chesham to Hyde Heath Common, and watched them into the Wheat Sheaf Inn, by the Devil's Den, Beech Wood, the property of Mr. Lowndes, of Bury House, Chesham. Beech Wood was more usually called "The Den." One of the men was believed to be James Keen, whom I have already spoken of. He it was who came and fetched me from the Chalk Pit, and he was formerly keeper to Mr. Fuller, under my father, but lost the berth because he was too fond of visiting the "Red Cow," the "Boot and Slipper," the "Wheat Sheaf," and other houses of call. He was now dressed up as a woman and wore pattens, but I knew him in spite of the disguise, and saw him go into the Wheat Sheaf. This inn was kept by Tom Stevens, a poacher's friend. He bred pheasants for gentlemen, to turn them (the pheasants, not the gentlemen) down in the woods, and also bought eggs and young pheasants from poachers.

Richard Lovering, an underkeeper, and myself were watching the young fowls, and my father was watching the pheasants. The chickens were in the pheasants' coops, and so were mistaken for pheasants by the poachers; the pheasants had been taken from the meadow up into the plantation, in White's Wood. Just after twelve o'clock, on Sunday night, we heard the men coming from the road; they went straight into the meadow, and took the chickens in the coops. Dick hailed them three times, and then fired his gun, which was a signal for father. They ran away towards White's Wood taking the chickens with them; father, hearing the signal, ran down from White's Wood. He met the poachers just as they were going through a trap gate in the hedge, into the third field from our house. He collared two, one in each hand, and then I arrived on the scene, old Dick following me up, rather slowly and reluctantly, about a hundred yards behind.

"Here we are, father; here's me and Dick. Catch hold of them, Dick," I cried. This was only bounce, as Dick had not yet come up, but he did so soon afterwards. I knew both the men my father held. One was Widdie Dell, and the other William Cogdill. Both were from Chesham, and, in fact, the same men whom I had seen buy the wire, some years before, and whom I afterwards met in Monk's Wood, when they enquired for their donkeys. The rest of the poachers got away, and ran across the standing corn; but Dell and Cogdill showed fight, and we had tough work with them. My father knew both men well, but he could not for the moment remember Cogdill's name. Cogdill was a tall, powerfully built man, and he refused to give his name, so my father let go of Widdie Dell, and, after a short tussle, threw the other, and then held him down. Dell was armed with a fold-stake, and the moment he saw his pal down he waved his weapon above my father, swearing that he would " smash his —— brains if he didn't leave go." It was just at this point that I arrived on the scene, and although it all happened more than fifty years ago, I can see it now in my mind's eye as I write.

There was father and Cogdill rolling on the ground, and Widdie Dell dancing round them, using fearful language, and working his stake like a thrashing flail, every stroke getting nearer my father. Father kept Cogdill down, and old Dick stood by, looking on, and doing nothing but shout from one to the other: " All we want is civility—all we want is civility." It occurred to me—though not apparently to old Dick—that we were in the wrong company to get civility. My father had put down his gun in order to collar the two men, and this I now took up.

"I know *you*, Widdie Dell," said my father, as he let him go, holding fast on to Cogdill, notwithstanding his struggles and the menaces of his companion. I had brought with me an old sword, which I had purchased from old Dick, he having been formerly a soldier, and now in receipt of a pension. He seemed to lose all his presence of mind; but as he was a man, and as I had my hands full with the gun—which was of course loaded—I called to him to take the sword, and then, as I was handing it over, the stupid old idiot allowed Widdie Dell to snatch it away. At this moment Cogdill began to shout: "Are you going to let me up? Let me up, you ——. I'm choking." In truth, my father was not a light-handed man, nor remarkable for gentleness.

"I'll let you up if you give your name," said he.

"James Barnes," in a hoarse gurgle.

"Where from?" asked my father.

"Charteridge." I knew he lied; but I had to keep moving round father to ward off Dell, trying all the while to rouse up old Dick to do something. The only success I met with in the last named direction was, that Dick kept on repeating: "All we want is civility." I could not help thinking that Dick was an ass.

Widdie Dell now dropped the sword, and, swearing horribly all the time, again flourished the stake about, and I half expected every moment that, although he might not smash out father's brains purposely, he might do so by accident. Meanwhile Cogdill kept urging him to beat father off. I regained possession of my sword, just as father let go of Cogdill; but he immediately seized him again, saying: "That's not your name. I know you, but I can't remember your name. Confound you."

Then followed a sharper struggle than before, and my father threw him again; but, as they were on the side of a bank, Cogdill gave a twist, and somehow got uppermost.

"Now," said he, "it's my turn." And with

that he caught father by the collar, and, jamming his knuckles into his windpipe, tried to strangle him. When I heard father gasping for breath and well nigh choking, I yelled at Dick to beat Cogdill off, but he only stood stupidly by, muttering: "All we want is civility." This so enraged me that I rushed at Cogdill, and struck him with my sword as hard as I could, repeated blows on his back, head and face. Then, finding that this made but little impression, I prodded his nether garments with the sword, which, fortunately, had a fairly sharp point. Cogdill gave a loud scream, and rolled off. Father called out to old Dick, and he, at last, did something holding the poacher down whilst father got up and regained his breath. This Dick managed easily enough, for he was a very strong and powerful man; and had he been blessed with any amount of pluck, very few men could have stood up before him for long.

Father now took the loaded gun from me, and, pointing it at Dell, said:—"Now, Widdie, you've threatened my life over and over again, and, if you don't drop that fold stake, I'll blow your arm off this instant." Thereupon Dell threw away the stake, without the slightest hesitation; and now it seemed probable that Dick would get what he wanted—a little civility, for Dell was one of the rankest cowards alive, and would cave in directly anyone sparred up to him.

"Are you going to let me up?" shouted Cogdill.

"Yes, if you give your right name."

"You know,——you; Will Cogdill."

"Let him go, Dick," said my father, and all five of us then went to the trap gate in the hedge, when Cogdill swore out:—"I should have done you, Luke, if it hadn't been for that confounded boy of yours." I laughed, well pleased; and so we reached the road, and parted.

The two poachers absconded, but, after a while, Dell returned and gave himself up to the parish constable, for there were no police at Chesham then. Dell split on his pal, and told the constable where to find him, at what hour of the night to go, and how they might best capture him. Acting according to his directions, the constables went to a certain Inn at Shepherd's Bush, kept by a widow named Jones. This widow had incontinently fallen in love with the burly poacher, and, at great personal risk, was now sheltering him from justice. Had it not been for Dell and his sneaking ways, she would have married William, and we should have had a pretty little tale to tell of the reformed poacher who married the innkeeper's widow, and kept the inn, making an excellent host, who lived happy ever after, and died at peace with all men.

It was half-past twelve at night when the constables reached the Inn, which was, of course, by this time shut up and dark; they rapped at the door. No answer. They rapped again, and again after that. Then at length the widow opened a front window and asked what they wanted. They answered, laconically, that they wanted the door opened. This was done, the widow seeing that they were constables, and that resistance would be useless; besides she thought they would never be able to find Cogdill, who had by this time got safely to his usual hiding place. To her horror and surprise, however, the constables went straight to the cellar and began to tap, with their staves, the barrels. At last they came to a huge beer cask, which sounded hollow and empty when rapped. "Sounds empty," quoth a constable, grimly. "Things is not always as they seem," remarked another, cheerfully. "Give us a leg up, mate." The cask was about seven feet high, and the men got a trestle, on which one of them clambered, and thus threw a light on the top. There was no covering, but inside stood a man, who instinctively turned his face up to the light. It was Cogdill himself. They got him out of the empty cask, the widow, meanwhile, weeping piteously and imploring "her Will" to "go quietly along with the gentlemen." He seemed disposed to follow her advice, and offered no resistance whilst they led him out, the constables bidding the widow "good night," kindly enough. The party came at last to a very steep hill, where they all got out of the cart and walked to ease the horse. When they reached the top of the hill, however, Cogdill obstinately refused to re-enter the cart, and the two constables could do nothing with him, until a brewer's cart came along, when they got the dray-man to help them. With his assistance, the poacher was bound hand and foot, drawn up into the cart, and thus conveyed to Chesham.

The two poachers were sent for trial to Aylesbury, where I, and father, and Dick Lovering had to appear as witnesses against them. They were tried before Sir Thomas Freemantle, found guilty, and sentenced to transportation for life Dell having been previously tried fourteen times, and convicted eleven, Cogdill tried eleven times, and convicted nine. Cogdill died going across the water, but Dell lived, and returned to Chesham forty years after, dying there in 1885.

I was at Chesham, on a visit, in '83, and called at Dell's house, but did not see him as his son-in-law said that he was ill in bed. I was told, afterwards, that Dell said that, if he had known it was I who had called, he would have killed me, if he swung for it; but that was only talk for talk's sake, on his part, for he heard me in the house, speaking with his son-in-law, and recognised my voice. The fact is that Dell was enraged at my returning to Chesham, even on a visit. My father was dead, I had left Chesham in '40, and Dick left soon afterwards, so that when Dell came back from abroad—a comparatively rich man, I believe—he declared that he had been wrongfully convicted, thinking that there would be none to speak to the contrary. I am no lawyer, but it seems to me that the case against them was as clear as could be; I knew both poachers, ever since I was seven years old, and recognized them that night in Monk's Wood, when they asked me about their donkeys. If they were innocent, why did they both bolt the very night that my father and Dick caught them? Why did Dell come home and give himself up to the Constables? Above all, why did Dell split upon his mate; a shabby piece of business whether he were guilty or not? Thus it is no wonder that Dell was enraged at my turning up again, and George Rose, a man who succeeded my father as head gamekeeper to Mr. Fuller, told me that Dell bragged to him that if he met me he would "kill me dead." This man, Rose, now lives at the Half-Way-House, where my father resided at the time when Dell and Cogdill were caught.

When I was visiting Chesham in '83, I came across an old mate of mine, who was formerly at the British School with me. He and I went to an inn to have a glass of beer together, and then he told me what Dell had been saying.

"Why," said I, "if my father swore falsely about him so did I, and Dick Lovering too, for we were all three witnesses, and swore positively to our men. Dell will want to make out that a man doesn't know his own wife next."

There were several men listening, and they believed my story, and repeated it broadcast; and so Dell's false tale was upset.

In conclusion, I may mention that the men who ran away that night were never caught. They threw down the birds as they were going over the standing corn, and the corn being in full ear the chickens kept themselves alive, and became quite wild. Mr. Fuller killed some of them whilst partridge shooting, in the month of September following, and father killed some in October and November, near Monk's Wood and Gold's Hill, whilst hunting the hedges for rabbits.

CHAPTER III.

CONCERNING TRAPPING, SNARING, AND OTHER MATTERS.

I WAS now employed in trapping and snaring rabbits, also hunting a pack of rabbit-dogs during the rabbit season, and going to various gentlemen's covers with my pack. I used frequently to go to Squire Carrington's, at Great Missenden Abbey, High Wood cover, Hyde Heath; and to Stonyfield, by Rook Wood, near the Abbey. Squire Carrington, when he had a big day's shooting on, always borrowed Mr. Fuller's rabbit dogs; and on such occasions

I, in my turn, used to borrow Squire Lownde's dogs, so that Squire Carrington used to get two packs of dogs and me into the bargain. Sometimes I used to go to Lord George Cavendish, who was afterwards Lord Chesham, at Latemore Park; Harry Highat was his head-keeper. Then sometimes I would go to Squire Drake's place, at Amersham; Pratt was his head-keeper; or to Lord Hampden, whose head-keeper was Butt; or to the Duke of Buckingham's place at Hampden Hullock.

My father and Pratt usually accompanied me, but I always hunted the dogs, and I understood them so well that I could excite them to run until they almost dropped dead from exhaustion. Many a time, after a hard day's hunting in the gorse, I have had to lay my coat on the ground and put two dogs on it, whilst I took two more up in my arms and carried them forward for half a mile; then I would come back for the first two, and so keep on repeating the operation until I got them safely home. When dogs are thoroughly tired out, you should warm their food, give them a good meal, and dry them well before the fire. If you neglect these precautions, and allow them to coil up and go to sleep before feeding and drying, you will find them in the morning stiff as an iron hoop, and quite dead. They die in their sleep, and one morning I found three dogs so, though these were certainly delicate dogs, one being a "fancy," and the other two Blenheim spaniels. The best dog to stand rabbit hunting in the gorse is the Scotch terrier crossed with the rabbit beagle; such a cross produces a rough, wiry-coated beagle, with the true beagle music in his voice.

We had two little beagles called Frolic and Fancy, and I have never seen any others like them; they were smaller than many cats, and their bones finer, whilst their ears were like wafers, and one could actually tie them underneath the mouth. They were not worth their keep for hunting in the gorse, and were really only fit to hunt on a lawn; but they were fit for any drawing room, being as neat as wax work, and as clean as a man's face freshly shaven. They were given to Mr. Fuller by a gentleman whose name I forget. Mr. George Carrington had some very good dogs, but one of the best I ever saw was a Scotch terrier, belonging to Mr. Edward Carrington; its name was Flip.

We usually hunted with Mr. Carrington's dogs, before lunch, and with mine, afterwards. When the dogs began to get a bit tired and slack, Mr. Carrington would shout for me:—"Here, John Wilkins, come and hunt these dogs, nobody else can do it properly." Then I would run forward, cap in hand, amongst the dogs, and talk to them:—"Here, she goes—loo loo there—look out forra'd;—look out sir—Hi Bustler boy—loo there." Old Bustler would scamper off in full cry, followed by the rest of the dogs; and, if there were any strange gentlemen present, they would run forward, with their guns ready, hollaing out excitedly:—"Where's she gone, boy?" Then Mr. George Carrington would laugh and stutter out:—"He's only exciting the dogs to hunt." "But you saw a rabbit didn't you, boy?" "Lor, no, sir," I would reply. "I only wanted the dogs to find one." Then Mr. George used to laugh the more, and I think he did it partly to make me "show off" and partly to "sell" his friends, for he himself pretended to believe that there was a rabbit, and would rush ahead as if to shoot it, whilst he knew all the time that it was only my humbug.

I will now say a few words about rabbit snaring and trapping. My father was a good trapper of rabbits and other vermin, but, as a snarer, he was no great shakes, so I had to do all the snaring. He was very hard on me; he gave old Dick a shilling a dozen for all the rabbits he caught, but I got nothing for mine, not even a penny a hundred. The more I did, the more he grumbled; so we did not get on very well together. If I said "yes," I was wrong for saying so; then I would say:—"Very well, father, I will say, 'no.'" And then he would abuse me for being a "turn-coat," as he called it. "All work and no play makes Jack a dull boy," and it was not otherwise with this "Jack." I would have gone through fire and water for him, if he had only given me a word of encouragement now and then, but this he never did, so I thought the matter out, and reasoned in this way :—"I try and do all I can to please you, and all I get in return is constant grumbling; if I do nothing for you, I can't get worse." So, as I had no peace, I resolved to declare war. It began in this way: he ordered me to take six dozen snares, go up a furrow in the wheat field stubble, and set every run that crossed the furrow. He had been growling at me, previously, and saw, I suppose, that my temper was soured; so he said, after he had given me my orders :—" I'll come and see that you set them well." I set them like clockwork, so that nothing could pass down the runs without being caught, and he came and inspected them when they were set. He told me next morning, to go and look at my snares, and, when I came home, after doing so, my mother said I was to go up to father's bedroom. Up I went, and found him in bed. "Well, sir," says he, "What have you caught? a dozen or more, I suppose." "Nothing," I answered, shortly. "Nothing?" echoes he, starting up. "Nothing, you tell me; there is nothing caught in your snares?" "Nothing," I repeated. "Ah! Master Jack, you are not going to get over me like that, I can tell you." He rolled out of bed. "I'll go and see for myself after I have had a bit of breakfast." So he did, and saw that there had not been a rabbit caught that night. He could not fathom this, at all; Jack had got the better of him in a draw of "blank."

Then he tried the oily feather, and this answered with me, "I say, my boy, do you think the rabbits would cross the wheat field stubble and get caught in your snares if we took out the dogs to hunt the gorse on Bishop's Hill?" The snares were set in the stubble, between two gorse fields, so I answered:— "Perhaps they might." But this I said, more because I wanted the fun of shooting, than anything else, for I knew that the rabbits would not go down to my snares. Why? Because they knew that the snares were there, for I had told them so, as I will explain later on; they had come down in the night, scented the snares, and gone away again, back to Bishop's Hill. Therefore, they would not go to the snares in the morning, for the wind was in the right quarter to blow the scent towards the gorse on Bishop's Hill.

We went home and fetched the dogs and gun, and he tried the experiment, but no rabbits crossed the stubble. I had thirteen shots, and killed twelve rabbits, and my father had twelve shots, and killed one only; but he thought more of his one out of twelve than I did of my twelve out of thirteen. We then went home to dinner, and I overheard father say to my mother:—" Jack can catch rabbits, or not, in his snares, just as he likes; I put him out, yesterday, before he went to set those snares, and not one rabbit was caught; yet the snares were set well I know, for I came upon him just as he was setting the last half dozen." Aha! father, the secret was not in setting the snares, for I could not do otherwise than set them properly, when he was looking on. Well, this little game made father very pleasant with me for a while, until he began to forget it, and then I had to wage war again, 'till he found out that it was his best plan to speak a little more kindly to his son, and give him a word of encouragement when he deserved it. I often deserved this word but seldom got it. It makes me recall old Dick's maxim:—" All we want is civility," and that I was not overpowered with by my father.

I have previously said that he was a man with a violent temper, and, when I was young, he used his walking stick pretty freely on my back, for very trifling offences. I remember, on one occasion, he accused me of doing something which he had really done himself, and he plied his walking stick across my back 'till his arm ached. I was about eleven years old at the time, and, when my father was about to give me dose two, Jim Keen, who was present and who knew that it was father's mistake, took off his coat, and said father must thrash him if he wanted to do any more thrashing. Now Jim had fought some of the leading fighting men, and always thrashed them, so father thought discretion the better part of valour, and I was let off. I never forgot Jim for that, and, when I afterwards became head keeper, I always used to send him five shillings, at Christmas, for his Christmas dinner, and my old keeper's coat. Mr. Benjamin Fuller and his keeper, George Rose, knew that I sent Jim a Christmas box, every year, but neither of them knew what it was for. It was a secret between myself and Jim, and he never told anyone, for he knew that I did not want to expose my father's faults whilst he lived. And now to hark back to the snaring.

My father told mother that he believed I had some artful dodge with my snaring, as I used a bit of wash leather to draw down the snares, in order to rub out any kinks or nicks in them, so that they should play quickly, and slip up like clockwork as soon as a rabbit got his head in. There was no scent on the wash leather, and I only used it for the purpose I am about to describe. Squire Drake's gamekeeper, Pratt, taught me to make and set snares, and put me up to the dodge about the wash leather. He, and father, and I were together, one day, in Monk's Wood, and Pratt set six snares, bidding me watch him attentively, which I did. "Now

Luke," said he to father, "I'll bet you a crown there'll be five rabbits out of the six snares, to-morrow morning, when John comes to look for them." He nodded and winked at me, and, sure enough, there were five rabbits caught, next morning. My father thought that Pratt had rubbed five snares with the leather and not the sixth, and he frequently asked me about "that bit of leather that Pratt used," thinking it a very bewitching thing for rabbits. Here father was wrong, for the leather had not much to do with it; but Pratt had picked out his six runs—"killing runs" as a good snarer would call them—very carefully. All good rabbit snarers should be very particular to have their hands very clean, and free from any smell of gun powder, rabbits' blood, paunches, dogs, or anything of that kind. This was why Pratt used the wash leather, to keep his hands from having actual contact with the snares, but the great secret of his success lay in the fact that he laid his snare in that part of the rabbits' run called the "rabbits' jumps."

Now, Pratt, on the occasion of which I am

speaking, had been shooting with my father, so his hands were more or less scented with gunpowder and blood; therefore he took up a handfull of mould from the ground, and well rubbed his hands with it, to take away the scent, and this he called "washing hands" before handling the snares. He then took the wash-leather, and pulled the wires into their proper shape, after having set the snare, without having actually touched the wire at all. My father had his own ideas about this leather, and clung to them with all an old man's tenacity; but he was wrong, for I could not use it either to draw or entice rabbits into my snares, but by not using it I could prevent, to a great extent, the rabbits coming near.

In setting snares, first wash your hands with soap and water, and then with some earth taken from the place where you wish to set the snares. This not only takes off the scent, but prevents your hands from getting clammy. Again, you should never set snares in the latter part of the day. Snares set in the morning catch twice as many rabbits as those

CONCERNING TRAPPING, SNARING, ETC. 47

set in the evening or afternoon, because the scent gets off and evaporates during the day, whereas in the evening the dews fall and preserve the scent freshly all night, thus warning off the rabbits. The same thing applies to trapping as well as snaring. I used to bet old Dick a shilling that I would beat him with twelve traps, and these were the terms of the bet: Dick was to go with me and see me set my traps, and then I was to go with him and watch him set his traps; and in the morning we were both to visit the traps together. We did so, and I always won; and Dick would say, "Well, I thought my traps were set as well as yours, Jack, but you've beaten me, that's certain." "Yes, Dick," I used to answer, "I told the vermin not to come near your traps, when you were setting them." Neither Dick or father could understand it at all.

My father was a better trapper than most, so I would say to him, "Now, father, you call yourself a first-rate trapper"—which he did, modesty not being the strong point in keepers; "I can beat you any day in the week, I know." Then he would set his traps, whilst I looked on and lent him a hand. "There, Jack," he says, after setting one very carefully, "you can't beat that, I know." And I instantly reply, "I'll bet you what you like that won't catch, if it stays there for a month." Nor did it; I took good care of that, for I had the chance of going to these traps as often as I liked, and so would "doctor" them, and cheat both father and old Dick. I used to play the same games with the snares, when at "war," as I called it, with my father. I would "doctor" certain traps, or snares, and bet that they would not catch, and they didn't; I would leave others alone, and bet that they would catch, and they did. It was wrong of me, I know, but I was very young at the time.

Father died without having ever found out the secret about the snares catching or not catching. He said it was just according to what temper I was in; but here he made a mistake, for it was just according to what temper *he* was in. My father got fourpence a head for all the vermin he killed, and he gave old Dick twopence a head for his; but I, who destroyed more than both of them together, got nothing. However, Dick gave me a penny a head for all my vermin, and as my father gave him twopence Dick got a penny, and I did the same; so that if father did not pay me directly, he paid old Dick for me instead.

CHAPTER IV.

CATCHING MY FIRST POACHER.

TRAPPING and snaring rabbits occupied us during the winter months, and in March vermin trapping—that is, the trapping of vermin other than rabbits—came on.

Pheasants begin to nest about the twentieth of April, and the poachers always had pheasants' eggs for sale at Chesham Fair, which was on the twenty-first. Along now is always a hard time for keepers, and I often had to be up and out by three o'clock in the morning. I was about fourteen or fifteen years' old when I first took charge of a wood, to look after all by myself. Father gave me my choice as to which wood or plantation I preferred to take,

CATCHING MY FIRST POACHER. 51

so I chose Monk's Wood. This wood is a great favorite with poachers, as it lay only one field from Weedon Hill Road and Coppeyson's Lane. A hedge came straight from the Chesham Road and the lane from Amersham Common, and from Weedon's Hill the road from Chesham to Hyde Heath Common went straight to Monk's Wood, so that poachers could steal along the road, covered all the way by the hedge. As I delighted in a good chase and a rough and tumble "scrap," I agreed to take Monk's Wood, and this father allowed me to do, because I was the best runner of the lot. The poachers always took to their heels, and bolted off for one of the roads I have named whenever they were disturbed. Father, however, would not always let me keep to my wood, but made changes in our beats. He sometimes took Monk's Wood, and sent me to Bishop's Hill, Old Wellington's Copse, and New Wellington's Copse, all three of which were adjoining, and formed one man's beat. This, too, was the best beat for poachers, next to Monk's Wood, as they could get into it by the other roads from Chesham to Hyde Heath Common, near by my father's house. They usually came up the Half Way House Lane, so called because it was half way between Chesham and Hyde Heath, near the Devil's Den. This lane parted the manor of Mr. Fuller from that of Squire Lowndes, and Coppeyson's Lane parted Mr. Fuller's property from Squire Drake's estate; but the poachers did not like this way so well as that which led to Monk's Wood, because they had to pass right by father's house, and that they particularly objected to. I begged my father to let me keep to my own favorite wood, and asked him why he changed me. "Are you not satisfied with me, father?" I said. "Oh, yes, Jack; it's not that." "Then why change my beat?" "Well, Jack," he answered, quite feelingly, "you are too venturesome with poachers, and I am afraid that they will harm you; I often tremble for your life. I shouldn't be a bit surprised if you were killed some fine day." I had always thought my father a hard and stern man, with but little love for me, but knew better from that time.

So I took his hand and pressed it warmly, and, having nothing to say, turned it off by a laugh. "Ah, John," my father went on, "You don't know your danger or you wouldn't be so venturesome, but I tell Matthew and Dick to run up to your call directly, when you are chasing poachers." Father need not have troubled about that, for I was quite sure that no Chesham man would hurt me, and, as a matter of fact, they never did, or attempted to. I don't know why, except that I was always rather a favorite with them; there was something about me they always liked, though what that something was I cannot tell. I think they rather admired my pluck, for, if I was in a fight, they always saw fair play, and backed me on to thrash my lad, saying;—"Go it Jack, my boy, you'll whip him like a sack, go it my little man o' war; here's your little Oliver, here's your little Napoleon." It was only from strangers that I had anything to fear in the way of ill-usage. I never had a blow from a local poacher in a public house row, it was only in a bona fide poaching affray that they fought me; when I was throwing them up, or taking nets or game away from them. When I was a young man I could turn out "in my skin" and have a fair stand up fight with any lad, and, on one occasion, I was bound over to keep the peace for twelve months, for fighting with Jack Weedon in Squire Lownde's Park. I was had up before the Squire and Mr. Benjamin Fuller, and father was bound over for me and Jack Weedon's mother for him; so this rather damped my fighting ardour, and made me feel somewhat ashamed of myself.

I went back to Monk's Wood, and left father to look after Bishop's Hill, and, one morning, when I was on the watch, I heard "scrunch scrunch" on the frozen beech leaves, and took up my gun ready for a shot, as I thought it was some kind of vermin on the prowl. Presently I saw a man step into the path, look round the bend, and then go back again to the edge of the wood. Here he knelt down, and began feeling about in the ferns. It was about half-past two in the morning, and I could only see the outline of the man as he groped on his knees.

I thought he was after pheasants' eggs, and made ready to catch him, taking off my coat and jacket, thus exposing my blue shirt sleeves. Then I crept up to within a few yards of my man, and, with a sudden spring, landed on his back, catching hold of his collar. He was a big strong man, and I thought I was in for a tough job, but I never saw such a total collapse in my life; the moment he felt my weight on his back he looked up at me, and then seemed to come all over limp. Half dragging him along to my gun, which I had left standing against a tree, I fired, and gave the 'dead holloa':—Whoo whoo whoop." Before we had turned out in the morning, my father had given us orders that, if either of us caught a poacher, he was to give this cry. "And you, Jack," said he, turning to me. "If you meet with anyone, fire your gun off before giving the holloa." Then, turning to the rest, he instructed them to run up to my assistance, immediately they heard my gun and call, throwing off their great coats, and divesting themselves of all impediments, for that purpose. The report of my gun acted on the poacher in a way I little expected; I cannot, from experience, describe the sensation of a "blue funk," but doubtless some of my readers have felt it, and I should think that my captive was in a blue funk, now.

"Let go, Jack," said he; "you know me well enough." But I still held fast. "Yes, I know you," I said: "still I want others to know you besides me." "Let go, will you," said the man, hoarsely; "Can't you see I am taken bad in my inside?" "All right, you may be bad or not, but, until someone comes up I don't leave go." It may sound heartless of me to talk like this, but keepers have to be up to all sorts of dodges. All this time old Dick and father kept answering my call, but the first to arrive was Matthew Atkins, and when he appeared I released my hold. Then old Dick came up. "Ah, Tom, my boy," says he, looking at the poacher, "you've got a good dose of physic this time." At this point we heard father call out, some hundred and fifty yards down the wood, and on our answering he shouted, "Go on; he's at the

White House by this time." Old Dick answered back, "Come here; we've got him here."

Up came father, with a flitch of bacon, four small loaves, and a jar of beer slung over his shoulder on his gun; and this in spite of his previous orders to us, about throwing off everything and running up to the first who called. In his fear of my getting hurt, he forgot these things, and so he came pounding along to where we were. He heard all we had to say, and then proceeded to search the poacher, whose name, it appeared, was Tom Tuson, although old Dick was the only one of us who knew him. Father could find nothing incriminating, however, so he said, "Now, Tom, I'll show you out of the wood." Then, as he walked him out, my father continued: "Why, how come you to let young Jack catch you? Didn't you run?" "Run?" growled the poacher; "by George, no. He sprung on me like a tiger, and I was never so unnerved in my life. What with his blue shirt and his long wavy hair, and the way he crouched down and sprang on me, I almost thought it was a tiger." It certainly was a bad light at the time, being just before daybreak, and so dark that he could not even see the eggs he was groping for amongst the ferns.

In a few moments father returned to us, and then old Dick tried him by "court martial," as he called it, for setting his men such a bad example, in acting contrary to his own orders. Dick constituted himself judge and jury, and solemnly found father guilty, fining him two gallons of Teddy Wheelan's ale, from Amersham brewery. Father paid up for the two gallons cheerfully enough, saying that he did not mind so long as "venturesome Jack" was not hurt. I may mention that I knew nothing of this Tom Tuson, and had never seen him before, nor have I set eyes on him since. Old Dick was the only one of us who knew him.

Tuson was summoned to appear before the magistrates, but absconded. I should explain that the "White House" that father mentioned was about half-way between Monk's Wood and Chesham, and he thought I was running my man down to the town from the wood. Mr. Benjamin Fuller had my name cut in the bark of the tree where I collared the poacher, and there it remained for some years, until the wood was cut down for timber to build a new farm house and other buildings at Weedon Hill, on the Doughty Tichborne farm.

This Tuson was known to be a good plucked 'un, and a rough fighting man, who would stand up for a good bout any day; but it must be borne in mind that he quite thought I knew him when I fired my gun. Had I not been so quick, and so frightened and unnerved him, he could have flung me into the gorse with the greatest ease, and made his escape, but fortune favors the brave, and, maybe, the rash. When we are up to evil and mischief, conscience makes cowards of us all, and poor Tom proved no exception to the rule. And thus ends the story of how I caught my first poacher.

I next went to Boxmoor, as keeper to the Right Honourable Granville Dudley Ryder, of Westbrook House, whose head keeper was Mr. Ball. I was living there when the first train ran from Euston to Boxmoor, and the line was afterwards carried on to Northchurch, and through the Northchurch tunnel.

At this time Ball was ill, so Mr. Ryder's butler came over to Chesham to see my father about me; the result being that I went to Boxmoor to look after the tame pheasants, on the understanding that, if Ball died, I was to take his place, but, if he recovered, I was to go back to my father. Ball did recover, I am glad to say, and was living at Boxmoor in March, 1885. Nothing of any interest occurred during the few months I held the situation, except that I shot some navvies' dogs. Some of these were beautiful dogs,—Bull terriers, Italian greyhounds, and some known as "plum pudding" dogs, being speckled and spotted all over, like a plum pudding.

The navvies used to come into the woods to look for me, and they would find their dogs dead, sure enough, but me they never caught. They would search in and around the trees and shrubs but could not find "the little devil"—meaning me—" or they would hang him in a

CATCHING MY FIRST POACHER.

tree by his heels," so I heard them say.

Whenever I shot one of their dogs I would take my gun and "shin" up a tree, and they used to come and prowl about under it, but never thought of looking up into it. The intellectual development of navvies, I may remark, is scarcely equal to their muscular development. So I was never found, and, even had they discovered my whereabouts, they could not have got me down, for I would have shot their fingers as fast as they climbed up.

During my stay at Boxmoor, an incident occurred which I must not omit to relate, as the poacher bested us all, including the magistrates; but, later on, I shall show how this smart card played into my hands and had to cut and run.

CHAPTER V.

"WHAT WAS IT?"

RICHARD Lovering, whom I have often mentioned before, was variously known as "Old Dick," "the Black Man of the Woods," "Wild Man of the Woods" and "the Black Devil." One evening, between six and seven o'clock, he came and told my father that the ride which parted Beech Wood from Owlett's Wood was set with snares for hares.

"Well Dick," said my father, "We must be there by nine or ten to-night, or else we shall lose our chance; it won't do to leave it 'till the morning." Dick thought that those who set the snares would not come to look at them until daybreak, and said so, but my father replied:—"I tell you, Dick, that they *will* come, and hunt the large clover field joining the wood where the snares are set, to-night, when they turn out of the public house; so we must be ready for them.

Off we went, accordingly, and father placed all three of us. I was stationed some hundred yards down the wood, between the snares and Chesham Common, to act as a stop, and catch anyone who ran away from old Dick, since he could run as well as a tame fat duck.

Just after the church clock struck eleven, we heard the voice of a dog in the clover field; he chased some hares into the wood, about a hundred yards below me, and they flew past the dog in "full cry" after them. Directly, however, the animal got scent of me, he stopped short, and ceased to give tongue, as if he had been shot dead, and all was quiet.

A few minutes afterwards father and old

Dick came up, and the former said:—"It's all up with us to-night, Jack; that dog of their's winded us, or we should have had them, right enough. They knew we were here, directly he stopped his voice in full cry. We shall never do anything with them 'till you get that dog, he is more use to them than any two men.

We may as well take these snares up," he added, turning to old Dick. But Dick thought that there was a chance that they might come at daybreak, as they had not seen any of us. Eventually, however, we resolved to act upon father's advice, and leave it 'till the next night.

So, the next night, we all three sallied forth and took up our positions, father and Dick in much the same places as the previous night, but having a due regard to the wind. I took my stand in an old saw pit, in which timber had been sawn some years previously, and which had not yet been filled up. This pit was just the right depth for me, as, when standing up in it, my chin was on a level with the ground; thus I was able to see all round out of the pit, and shoot the dog, did he appear.

"Now John," said my father, in parting, "Sit down 'till you hear the dog coming, and mind you don't rise up 'till he gets near enough for you to make sure of killing him. If you are too eager he'll wind you, but if you let him get near enough for a dead shot, it don't matter whether he winds you or not; stops, goes forward, or turns back."

"All right, father," said I. "I'll manage it, I'll be sure to kill him, never fear."

"I'm not afraid but what you will," said father. "But if you don't keep down close, he'll be sure to wind you, and I'd rather have that dog than all the poachers, so don't you miss this chance."

I may mention that there is nothing so trying to a keeper as a poacher's dog, it seems to be imbued with more than the cunning of its masters, and the instinct seems more trustworthy than their reasoning powers. It is always distrustful of strangers and, in fact, everybody except its masters, and enters at once into the keen delight of the lawless deeds of the latter; at the same time it is quick to suspect danger and scent an enemy, its instinct prompting it not only to save itself, but also to give warning to its owners, that they may do likewise. I have known a whole gang of poachers broken up for the season merely by the loss of their dog, and thus keepers are always death on dogs, so it should not seem cruel if they shoot all strange dogs found in the covers.

It was a bright moonlight night, and I sat in this old saw pit for about two hours and a half without seeing or hearing anything, when, all at once, I became aware of something at the end of the pit jumping and dancing about, here, there, and all over the place. It came up to the side of the pit, very close to my head, and then disappeared, suddenly, like a bladder bursting. Next I saw it hanging on the side of a tree; it left the tree, though I could not see it do so, but immediately reappeared skipping round the pit. I could not make it out at all; at first I thought it was an owl, and then I remembered that an owl would fly and not hop, skip and jump. Last of all, the thing hung on to a branch of the tree, in the full light of the moon; I forgot all about snares, and dogs, and poachers, and father's orders, and simply let fly at it, determined to find out what it was. Nothing fell, nothing flew away, the result was just the same as if I had shot at a bubble; indeed, the thing itself was just like a soap bubble that a child might blow through a long clay pipe. It was as large as a common—or garden—hen, but shaped something like a pig's bladder blown out, and, when I had shot, it seemed as if all the wind had escaped.

Up I jumped out of the pit, and rushed up to the tree to pick up what I had shot, for, though I saw nothing fall, I am a pretty dead shot, and I scarcely believed I had missed my quarry. Nothing there; neither fish, flesh, fowl, or even a feather. Father and Dick now arrived, and found the gun standing in the pit, and me, alternately, gazing up into the tree, or groping on the ground.

"What did you shoot at?" growls father.
"Something," I replied, feebly.
"Well what was it?"

"Something," was all I could say, again, dubiously staring at the tree, or feeling the ground, all the while.

"What was it you shot at?" insisted father.

"I don't know."

"Well, what was it like?"

Then I told them how it jumped here and there, and appeared and disappeared, all around me; whereupon my father up with his hand, and gave me a heavy clout over the side of my head.

"You cracky," he raved. "You shot at the shadow of the moon; now you've spoilt the job entirely."

So he took up the snares and we all went home, he grumbling and growling all the way, and I was very glad to get to bed out of his sight, I can tell you.

Next morning, Dick and I went to examine the place by daylight to see if we could find any trace of what I had shot at; needless to say, we searched in vain, I could see that I had shot just were the thing was, for there were the marks in the tree. I think it must have been what they call a " Will o' the Wisp," or " Jock o' Lantern," that is, a kind of vapour; I had never seen one of them before, but I've seen plenty since.

CHAPTER VI.

HARRY WRIGHT'S SANDY RABBIT.

OLD Dick came home, one night, and told my father that he had again found a hedge set with snares, at the bottom of the clover field. This was the same field where I had stood in the saw pit, and shot at the moon. I hear that people shoot the moon, nowadays, some times.

We all three went out that evening to watch the snares, I being again placed, as a stop, at the end near Chesham. We remained watching until after eleven o'clock, and then father came up to me, and said:—"We'll give it up now, and go home and have something to warm us." We wanted something of that kind, for it was a rime frost, and one of the coldest nights I was ever out in. So we went home, and thawed a bit before a big fire. We had some hot coffee, bread and home cured bacon; and then father and Dick smoked their pipes, and drank home brewed ale, whilst I dropped off to sleep.

About half-past three we started out again, but, when we reached the hedge, the snares were gone. Now, on the previous day, father and I had been rabbiting with the nets, as he had an order for three dozen live rabbits, which we duly caught. When old Dick told us about the snares, father took one of these rabbits with him, having previously marked it so that he would know it again. I was carrying this rabbit when we started out first, and, by some means or other, it got out of my pocket, and was caught in one of the snares set in the hedge. We had left it in the snare when we went home to have a little refreshment, and, when we arrived on the scene a second time, it was gone, and all the snares too. So we returned home again, having drawn a blank.

Three or four nights after this, my father went into a public house, to pay the landlord for a pig he had bought off him, and, incidently, to have a drink. Whilst he was there, the landlord took down a rabbit from off a hook, and, holding it up, said:—

"There, Luke, you can't get rabbits like that."

Father took it and examined it, pronouncing it to be one of the best he had ever seen. "I should like to get some of that stock to turn down in White's Wood gorse," said he, carelessly. "Where might it come from?"

"I don't know where it come from," replied the landlord. "But I bought it off Harry Wright, the miller, last Tuesday."

This was the very rabbit I had lost out of my pocket, so we then knew all about it, for the hedge where the snares were set was only one field from Harry Wright's mill. On enquiring, we learnt that Wright took night turns with another man, at the mill, he on, one night, and the man on, the next; the night we lost the rabbit was Harry's night on, so that accounted for our losing it in the dead of night.

This miller was a perfect torment to old Dick, he could scarcely ever prosecute him, and, when he did, never got him convicted, as Harry was a most artful card, and clever both at poaching and the law.

Dick saw him, one time, shoot a hare on the fallow, in the mill field, and put it in his pocket. Wright was taken before the Magistrates, Mr. Lowndes and Mr. Fuller, and, when Dick had given his evidence, they asked Harry if he had anything to say.

"Yes, gentlemen," said he, politely. "I have a great deal to say. I am quite sure, gentlemen, that the witness Lovering don't intend to say anything but what's true, but he is labouring under a mistake, as I will prove to you if you'll allow me. I have three witnesses to call, who will prove my case. Now, I keep a lot of tame rabbits, amongst them a large sandy buck that I keep for stock; I don't keep him in the hutches with the does, but let him run loose in the rabbit house. The door of the house was left open, one day, and my buck goes out and gets under the wood stack which joins the rabbit house, where I kept on trying to catch it, but without success. It had been out for six or seven weeks, and as it had been continually hunted, got very wild; so, on this very day, I set about moving the wood stack, in order to get at it, when it ran across the road into the mill field fallow, and squatted down."

"I said:—'Call in the dog, don't let him go after the rabbit, as I can get it now. I'll just shoot it, so mark the place where it squatted, while I go and fetch my gun.' Well, I did so, and shot it, and here's the rabbit to prove it." With that he pulls a large sandy rabbit out of his pocket. "And here," he went on. "Are two—no, three witnesses who saw me shoot it." Harry was as good as his word, and had no difficulty in proving that he had really shot the rabbit; so he had, but it was undoubtedly after he had shot the hare.

Old Dick swore to the hare, and I have no

doubt, in my own mind, but what he was right; however, the magistrates gave Wright the benefit of the doubt, and dismissed the case. Thereupon Harry went to the public house, and bragged how he had licked old Dick, and the magistrates as well; true enough he had licked them, clean and handsome, but he got into different hands afterwards, when "young Jack" got hold of him, for I licked him quite as fairly as he did old Dick, as I will show, later on.

CHAPTER VII.

THE END OF POACHER BOB.

AS I have mentioned before, Ball, Mr. Ryder's head keeper, recovered, so I went back to father, when Mr. John Fuller said he was afraid that I should never be big enough for a keeper, and that I had better be apprenticed to a shoemaker. Father, too, used to sneer at me, and said:—"All you are fit for, Jack, is to stand behind a counter and tear up calico." Then he would put his hands together, and make a noise with his mouth, as if he were tearing a piece of calico in two. So I decided to try my hand at something else for a while, until I could get a place as under keeper, for a keeper I determined to be.

I left Hyde Heath and went to Lord Dormer's place at Little Kingsvale, near Peterby House, between Great Missenden and Wickham Heath, on trial as a carpenter. I did not stop long, however, and went from there to Great Berkhampstead with Lord Dormer's son, to try sawing in Mr. Key's wharf yard there. I spent one summer at Berkhampstead, and went in for charcoal burning at Pengrove, near Beech Wood, which is about the centre of the manor. There had been a large fall of timber at Pengrove, and Mr. Fuller gave me leave to burn my charcoal in the wood so as to save carting it to Hyde Heath Common.

Whilst I was thus burning charcoal, poor old Dick fell ill with a bad leg, and the Chesham doctors said that he would never be fit for his work again, so he had to keep at home with his leg. Mr. Fuller asked me to "look out" whilst Dick was laid by, and this I was able to do because I had employed a regular charcoal burner to burn for me, and he kept by the fire when I used to be travelling round to London, Oxford, and other places, for orders.

I had not been in old Dick's place long before I came across a hedge set with snares. This hedge ran from the New Road to Odds Wood, adjoining Hangman's Dell, and these snares were the means of bringing Poacher Bob to his death. On Thursday morning, while I was watching, I saw Jack Nash come and look at the snares, and, finding that they had caught nothing, go away again. I watched them off and on 'till Sunday morning, and then I saw Nash and another man come and look at the snares. A rabbit had been caught in them on Friday night, and there it still remained but the two men did not attempt to touch it, and went off down to the water side at Chesham. I watched them go to George Jones' house, which they entered, and subsequently came out again with Jones. Then all three went to Jones' barn, opened the door, and let out a dog; I recognized this animal as being the same that I intended to kill on the night when I shot at the moon. The party now went up, past Jones' house, to the Hangman's Dell, where the snares were set. I could see all this from

THE END OF POACHER BOB.

where I was, and now I heard them send the dog round to look for me; first here, and then there, saying :—" Try for him, good dog." They peered into the badger's earth close by, looked into the chalk pit, searched the roof of the hay-stack and all round it, and then sent Bob up the side of the hedge where the snares where set to look for me, once more. On arriving at the end, the dog looked back at the men, as if for further orders, when Jones called to him to " go over;" he thereupon jumped the hedge and came down the other side, all the way to the chalk pit, where the men stood. I heard them say that it was alright, and one of them immediately made for the rabbit and took it out of the snare, when to their surprise I appeared. On seeing me, the man with the rabbit gave leg bail towards Fox's Mill and Chesham, the route by which they had come. I made chase, and caught up with him after a run of a couple of hundred yards or so, only to find that he was a stranger to me. He refused to give me his name, and kept on walking towards the town, I keeping up with him.

When we reached Foxe's Mill, an old woman came out to fill her kettle at the pump; then another one came out to her door, to let down a shutter; then a third came out of another cottage, and the moment she saw us, she cried out :—

"Oh, dear neighbour, here's Charlie Coughtrey caught; young Wilkins has got him, poor Charlie's caught right enough." And away she goes next door. "Neighbour Jeffrey, poor Charlie Coughtrey's done for; look, young Wilkins has got him."

Then they all left their kettles and shutters and things and joined in a chorus of lamentations. "Poor Charlie, its all up with him now, or young Wilkins wouldn't be with him; poor Charlie.

"Good morning, Charles," said I, politely, and went back to the Dell, where I met the other two men, Nash and Jones.

"Well," they said, jeeringly, "now you've caught him you don't know him."

"What," said I, with feigned surprise. "You may as well say I don't know you two,

THE IDENTIFICATION OF "COUGHTREY, THE POACHER," BY THE OLD WOMEN OF THE VILLAGE.

as say I don't know Charlie Coughtrey." Then how they stared at each other!

"By gum," they growled. "He does know him after all."

All three men were summoned, but Coughtrey did not appear, and I have never seen him from that day to this. Jack Nash employed a Mr. Chester, a lawyer who had just taken an office at Chesham, to defend him. Nash had told him that he had never been out of the footpath at all on that morning, but when Mr. Chester heard my evidence—how I had seen Nash, on the Thursday previous, come and look at the snares, and then again on Sunday morning with Coughtrey, how I had heard Nash say that he wouldn't take the rabbit, as old Dick had caught him snaring rabbits before, and he wasn't going to be caught again,—then, after he had heard all this, and Mr. Garrett, of Chesham, swore that there was no footpath, and produced a map of the land to prove it, Mr. Chester addressed the magistrates saying that he was sorry he had taken up the case. He had, he said, been deceived by Nash's false tale, and all he could do was to recommend his client to the mercy of the bench. Nash was convicted, and got six months.

When we came out of court, there were about thirty poachers and roughs hanging about, with hats in their hands, ready to throw them—hats, not hands—up in the air and shout " hurrah." Some did begin :—" Hoo-hoo—," and then stopped off, dead, as they saw my father, Nash, and the constables come out. Nash was bellowing like a twelve-year-old child, and wailing out that he should never live through it. The gang of roughs slunk off, like so many dogs with tin kettles tied to their tails. It was a sad disappointment, for they all thought that Lawyer Chester was going to get his man off. And so, covering his face with both hands, and booing like a baby, Nash went off to gaol.

Jones begged hard to be let off: he said he would give up poaching, and never cause any more trouble. He brought his dog, the celebrated Bob, tied him up to Mr. Fuller's gate at the German House, and there blew out his brains; so Mr. Fuller let the case against him stand over and Jones did not go to gaol. This Bob was a big, rough, wiry, coarse-coated dog,—a cross between a blood hound and a sheep-dog, with the true voice of a hound. I do not know, for certain, his real breed, but I do know that he was the cleverest poacher I ever met.

Jones never did any poaching after this, and his wife repeatedly told me that she was glad I caught him; it was the best day's work that ever happened to him, she said, for he used to waste his time in poaching, and would then go to the public house and spend all the money he had earned by it, and a shilling or two beyond. "Easy come, easy go," and it did not end there, for he used to get drunk and was fit for nothing the next day, so he must needs go and have another quart, the next morning, to liven up yesterday's beer. This, again, very often led to a third day's drunk, and then the three days had to have a livening up on the fourth morning. Three or four day's loss of work at four shillings a day, two shillings a day for drink, say three days—a total of eighteen shillings loss. "And now," said she. "He sticks to his work, earns double the money he did, and don't spend a quarter he used; best of all, John, I get it now, but before, the public house got most of it."

When we all came out of the court, Mr. Fuller took father and me up to his house, and into the kitchen. He gave the cook orders to give us the best dinner she could, and with his own hands, he brought me a thumping big glass of hot brandy and water. Then he fetched me his own great coat and said, giving it to me:—"Now, John, I've got another job for you, so take this coat, and make as good a fist of it as you did with Nash."

CHAPTER VIII.

DABBER HARDING AND OLD SARAH.

THIS was a snaring job, which my father had found out. Having received my instructions, I left German House, and walked about two hundred yards to the back of the town, where there was a long strip of a plantation; into this I dived and, at the end of it, came upon a quick-set hedge full of snares. These I watched for about two hours, when a man called Dapper or Dabber Harding appeared, carrying a gun, and proceeded to beat the plantation up and down. After looking through it carefully he came and examined the snares, and then made off towards Odd's Wood. Father had given me orders to stay by the snares till he came, so I remained there until he arrived at about half-past five in the evening. I told him what had occurred, when he said:—

"I saw Dabber, with Harry Wright, round Odd's Wood and Old Beech Wood Lane, but could not get hold of them; but you'll be sure to nab Dabber at these snares, in the morning, and, if not, we can have him for trespassing in the plantation with a gun, and for setting snares."

Now, on my way to the plantation, I picked up a dead hare in the swedes, near Granlet's plantation; it had been killed quite long enough, and was just beginning to 'turn,' for the rooks had plucked out one eye, the lights and heart, so I hid her in the plantation for the ferrets. When I reached home with father, it struck me that I might make use of her in another way, so I borrowed a needle and thread from mother, and sewed up the places where the rooks had been picking; then I started her only eye hard out of her head, and smeared it round with blood to make it look blood-shot. I took old Sarah, thus prepared, and laid her, best side upwards, blind side downwards, in one of the snares I was watching.

Now poachers are very knowing and suspicious fellows, so that, when you are baiting a trap for them, don't despise your enemy and think that anything is good enough to take him in; you must meet cunning with ditto, and, to show you what I mean, I will describe very carefully how I 'faked' this dead hare.

I tucked her head in the noose and drew it moderately tight, then I took the slack of the wire and see-sawed it against the stems of the "quick" to rub the bark off, pulled out the fluck to show where she had torn herself when dashing about, and scraped up the leaves and moss to show where she had scratched and kicked about in the snare before she died. So, having completed my preparations, all I had to do was to wait and watch. About seven in the morning arrives Dabber with his gun, and beats the plantation down to where the snares were set; when he got within fifteen or twenty yards he saw old Sarah, and, dropping his gun, he rushed forward and fell flat on top of her. He took her out of the snare and pocketed her, whilst still lying flat on the ground; then he got up and carefully removed every scrap of fluck, after which he went back a little way into the wood, kicked up the moss and earth, and buried the fluck underneath, stamping it down out of sight with his feet. Next he took some earth and rubbed over the white thorn bush, in the place where the snare had barked it; then he brought some leaves, and strewed over the place where Sarah had scratched up the earth under the snare. After this he put up the quick, and made everything look as if it had not been disturbed; then, standing a little way off, he took a good view, and, coming back, placed a twig here and there, and smeared a little dirt over a spot in the bark that showed white. At last he seemed quite satisfied, and, indeed, one might have passed the place without ever noticing that anything had been recently caught there.

Off he goes with one-eyed Sarah, and, after going about twenty yards or so, he thought he'd take a peep at her. Just as he was doing this I stepped up behind him, on tiptoe, saying:—

"How is it? a good one, Dabber?" He sprang over the hedge into the road, and had reached his father's house before I could follow; here he ran to earth with both gun and hare. "Hum," thought I as he disappeared. "If I don't look out this will be another tame sandy rabbit job; he'll be after bringing some of his workshop mates, to swear he was in his workshop from five 'till eight this morning." So I went straight to the workshops, up by Chesham waterside.

As soon as I reached the timber yard I found two sawyers hard at work, near the entrance, and the moment the top-sawyer caught sight of me he sang out:—

"Whoa, stop, you there!" Then turning to his mate he said:—"Here's a lark, Dabber's done for a crown; ain't he Jack?"

"Yes," said I. "He's all right."

I proceeded to walk up the yard, when, one after another, the men came out of the workshops, saying:—

"Dabber's caught, for a shilling; ain't it so Jack?"

"Has he been here this morning?" I asked.

"No," says one.

"Yes," said a lot of voices together, all chaffing and laughing.

"Well, mates," said I. "Here's his bench, and he ain't here; where is he?" For I knew Dabber's bench. They commenced their chaff again, and one said that "Dabber had just gone out, as I came up, to get a half pint; he must have gone out the front way and seen me coming, and perhaps, made off, thinking I was after him." All this was said in chaff, the men winking at each other, but I began to think it looked rather queer for me, because if Dabber appeared then there were a dozen men ready to swear he'd been in his shop all the morning, and the rest would hold their tongues.

At this moment, however, Mr. Webb, the master, appeared.

"What's all this noise about?" he demanded. "John Roberts, go on with your work, and all the rest of you do the same." Then, turning to me, he said:—"What do you want here, Wilkins?"

"I want to know if Dabber Harding is here, sir, and, if not, whether he has been here this morning at all." On this, he looked into Harding's shop and found it empty, turning to the men, he said:—

"Mind, I will have no nonsense; has he been here this morning?"

"No, sir," replied the men, gravely enough now.

"You hear, John?" said Mr. Webb to me.

"Yes, sir, and thank you, sir," I replied.

I went off down the yard, and there was no running fire of chaff now, everybody seemed too much engaged to mind me. I turned up the alley leading into the street, and just as I was rounding, ran full butt against Dabber.

"Good morning, John," said he.

"Good morning, Dabber," said I. "Though we've met before, to-day, it ain't ever too late for civilities." He stared at me doubtfully for a moment, and then hurried down the alley. He was full run, and winded when I met him, and, had I not got beforehand with him, there is no doubt he would have brought any number of men to swear that he'd been at his shop all the morning.

All this occurred on the day after Nash was tried and convicted, and Harding was a leader of the roughs who waited outside the court to make a demonstration, if Nash had got off.

Harding was summoned but, the night before the day of his trial, they had a " free and easy " with one-eyed Sally. They cooked her, and made a supper off her at a beerhouse, and all the guests pronounced her to be beautiful eating. After having devoured poor Sarah, they fell to drinking beer, and this so warmed the cockles of their hearts that they made a collection for Dabber, who collared the offertory, took his hook next morning, and failed to answer to his summons. The day before I caught him he was waiting outside the court, hat in hand, ready to throw it in the air and cheer lustily, if Nash got off—such is life! Mr. Fuller gave me ten shillings for catching Dabber, with which I was well pleased, and praised me warmly for my shrewdness, with which I was still better pleased.

CHAPTER IX.

CONCERNING DICK AND OTHER THINGS

THE poachers about Chesham used to simply play with old Dick, he never caught one except by accident, and when he did he could never get his man convicted. He was no good for watching snares, being always beaten; he had no patience, and it often happened that, when a hare or rabbit was in the snares, the men would not touch it as they suspected that the place was watched. Then old Dick would come out of his hiding, and blackguard them, calling them all sorts of names and taunting them with their want of courage, but of course they only laughed at him and made off. Thereupon Dick would go away, grumbling and growling, thinking it of no use to watch the snares any longer. Of course the men were only lying in wait, and, the moment he had gone, they came and took any game that might be in the snares, for he often forgot to remove what was caught, or else he left it purposely, hoping to find it there still on his return, to act as a bait for the poachers. The latter soon got to know Dick's lazy and careless ways, and so bested him. Dick never ought to have been a keeper; he had no cunning about him, no tricks of dodging his men, changing his beats, and altering his clothes. He used to be just wound up like a clock, and I could always tell where to put my hand upon him at any given time of the day. As I have before mentioned, he was an old soldier, and had the discipline of the barracks thoroughly instilled into him, but although that is a very good thing in its way, it does not fit a man for the calling of a keeper. A keeper's life is one of continual strain and anxiety, and he must be able to adapt himself to all sorts of strange circumstances, in order to overcome the innumerable difficulties that arise in the course of his career. It is no child's play, I can tell you, for a thousand and one things occur that call forth all the talent and resource that a man possesses, in order to deal with them successfully.

For instance—a keeper has to rear ground game and flying game, a very difficult job, in which he has everything against him almost, and only the ordinary course of nature to assist him. The condition of the elements, flying vermin, ground vermin, and, lastly, man in the poacher shape, are all against him. During the rearing season the keeper never has any leisure at all, his hours are all the time; there are no definite rules which can be laid down for his guidance, and he can only fall back on his own common sense and tact. But to return to Dick.

He had just one round, like clockwork; he would go once through Beech Wood and then that would be done for the day, and he would not go near it again until the next day at precisely the same time. From Beech Wood he used to go to Odd's Wood adjoining Bois' Wood, Odd's Wood being on one side of a hill and Bois' Wood on the other, with a ditch between them. On the top of Bois' Wood is a summer house, and here old Dick used to arrive, about one o'clock every day, to have his dinner and a pipe under shelter. "The daily round the common task," was ever the same with Dick, and one day was like another, as one green pea resembles another green pea.

I used to dodge into a wood at one end, one time, and at another end, another time, making it a rule never to go the same way twice. Then, too, I constantly changed my dress, impersonating all kinds of people—mechanics, carpenters, and the like. A favourite dodge of mine was the carpenter 'fake'; I used, for this, to wear a white apron and a blue jacket, or, sometimes, a white flannel jacket, and to carry with me a carpenter's flail, handsaw, and axe. Sometimes I would go as a tramp with matches to sell, and sometimes as a ploughboy, wearing a white smock, going home with his bundle. It was almost always necessary to resort to some dodge of this kind in that part of the country, it being a most convenient place for poachers, and dead against keepers. The country was so open that men could see a great distance, and warn their mates on the approach of a keeper. When I 'made up' in any of my characters I took care to 'make up' my face as well, and many a time I have passed my friends in the road, or been amongst them in the market place, without ever being suspected; so I usually managed to pick up the information I wanted. To return once more to Dick.

The poor old chap had to 'cave in' owing to his bad leg, and Mr. Fuller gave him a sort of 'say so,' which, with his pension, enabled him to take a public house in the neighbourhood. Mr. Fuller then offered me Dick's place, and I took it, so there I was, in spite of what my father and Mr. Fuller had said about me,—a gamekeeper.

CHAPTER X.

DICK'S GHOST.

BEFORE old Dick gave up, he had repeatedly declared to father and me that he had seen a ghost near the Devil's Den. He said that you could neither see or hear it coming until it slid by; but it was just like a calf, made no noises, but glided along as if on skates. He had met it three or four times, just about the same place, and he got so nervous that he would not go past the Den on his way home at night.

One Sunday night, father had gone to Hyde Heath Chapel, and I was at home keeping

DICK'S GHOST. 99

mother company, when, all on a sudden, the dogs in the yard broke out barking madly. I slipped on father's list slippers, snatched up my gun, and went out to see what was the matter with the dogs. There was old Dick's ghost, clearing out of the yard like a streak of lightning it was just going through the folding gates, having to stoop down to get under, when I let fly and bowled it over, stone dead, without a sound save the report of "Brown Bess," my gun. Then I got my mother to help me drag it into the house, and cover it over with two sacks, under the salting trough.

When father came home, I said I would show him old Dick's ghost.

"Well,' said he, "I hope you may, Jack."

So I took him up to the trough, and pulled the sacks off the ghost. He stepped back in amazement.

"Sure enough, you've killed him, my boy," said he. "We'll leave him 'till the morning for old Dick to have a look at him, and then we must put him out of sight, as there will be a great stir as soon as he is missed."

When Dick made his appearance, next morning, my father said:—

"Jack shot your ghost, last night, Dick."

"Sure enough if he has I'll stand treat," replied Dick.

So we took him to the trough, my father first locking the front door, and then I removed the sacks and displayed the ghost. Old Dick nearly jumped out of his skin, exclaiming:—

"Ay, that's him, sure enough."

The ghost was nothing more than an enormous deer hound, and the highest dog I ever met. I had seen him once with his master, a farmer who lived on Hyde Heath Common, and, on that occasion, the dog caught a rabbit. As he was never kept on the chain he became a confirmed poacher, so I was not at all sorry for what I had done.

We took the body up to Bishop's Hill gorse, that night, and put him in a pit in the gorse; and there his bones are now, or rather, the bone dust, for it is more than fifty years ago. Dick read the burial service over him, and recited a poem of his own composition, over the grave.

The elegy ran something like this :—

"As you appeared from out the Den of Devil's Wood,
"And as you scared me often by the Devil's Den,
"We lay you here in Bishop's Dell, for good,
"To scare me no more, for ever. Amen, amen."

At the end of each line old Dick struck the ghost a vicious blow with his stick, and wound up with a series of blows, at the end of the ceremony. There was an end of Dick's ghost, and I never heard any more about it until one evening when father and I were in the "Red Cow" public house. Then the owner of the dog came in, and I heard father, in the course of conversation with him, ask what he had done with the deer hound, as he had not seen him since he had poached the rabbit by the Den.

"No," replied the farmer, "I sent him to my brother in Norfolk."

Father and I, on hearing this, looked at each other, but neither said anything.

Dick Lovering was not a very old man, having enlisted in the army at the age of seventeen, and served twenty one years. After being at home for two years, he took the underkeeper's place, being then just in his prime and full strength, and a very strong man he was. When he developed his bad leg he went to the Hemel Hempstead Infirmary, and Sir Astley Cooper cured him, so, when I went into Wiltshire, he came under my father again. Although his leg was cured he was not much good for anything except light work, such as pruning young Scotch Firs, and Birch, and "looking out," occasionally. So after a little while, as I have before stated, he took a public house at Hyde Heath.

Old Dick had a great many good qualities; he would call you at any time of the night you liked, as true as the clock, and you could always depend—and so could the poachers—on him to be at his post at any hour of the day or night. "Military time" with old Dick, always, punctual to the tick, and his appearance was something, for he was a great big man, and looked an awkward customer to tackle. I think I have delicately hinted, before, that he was not over endowed with pluck, otherwise he would have been foremost in every poaching fray.

All he wanted was 'civility,' and I am afraid poachers leave that at home when they are after your game.

CHAPTER XI.

HARRY WRIGHT CAUGHT IN A TRAP.

I HAVE before mentioned Harry Wright, and told you how he weathered old Dick, and the whole bench of magistrates, with his sandy rabbit trick. Master Harry used to go about the place bragging that no one could catch him; he met me in a public house, once, and taunted me to my face that I had not brains enough to take him. He said, moreover, that if ever I did he would be the death of me, but this was all mere idle talk, and so I told him at the time. Nevertheless, he was a very artful man, and a most determined poacher, and had given us a great deal of trouble, but there, as I said before, anyone could get away from old Dick.

Poaching, if pursued systematically and cleverly, is a good paying game, especially in the nesting season. There are always plenty of receivers of poached game and eggs, who give a fair price, and manage their business in such a manner that, although you can swear positively that the game and eggs came from your beat or wood, yet you cannot lay hold of them. The only way to catch a poacher is to take him red-handed. In the locality where I was under-keeper, there were paths (rights of way) running alongside the woods, and sometimes through them, and these rendered it doubly difficult to catch poachers, in such a manner as to lead to a conviction. It is of no use to search a man on one of these paths, unless you have actually seen him use that path for trespassing in pursuit of game; otherwise you search him at your own risk. You can summon him if you see him leave the path and go into the wood, or if you can catch him red-handed, that is, in the act of taking game, or with game about his person. The great thing is to make your 'catch' a certainty; a man may, whilst on the path, look at snares, but, although you know that he is a poacher, you cannot get him convicted unless you have actually seen him handling the snares. Then, again, you must know the man, and be sure of his name; if there be any doubt as to his name or actions, the benefit of it will not be on your side.

Now Harry Wright had a most artful way of going to work. He used to take his father's maid servant, and a man called George Harding, out with him, and, when he was on the poach, George used to walk thirty or forty yards behind, and the maid servant some way in front, so as to guard him both ways. If any of us came across him he had plenty of warning from one or other of the guards. This George Harding was a brother of Dabber's, and a basket maker by trade, and, although he lived near the mill, he had nothing to do with it. The girl was engaged to be married to Wright, and was almost as artful as he; she usually carried some flowers in her hand, and sometimes she would take a blackbird's nest with the eggs in it, or even the young birds. Thus it was a difficult thing to catch Harry, as he always made the excuse, if you came upon him searching for pheasant eggs among the briars, that he was only gathering flowers for his sweetheart, or else he was after a blackbird or thrush's nest, or a bullfinch to cross with his canary. Harry always did all the poaching himself, but sometimes the maid assisted him in looking for pheasant's eggs, in this way. Getting into a patch where a lot of flowers were growing, she would walk about, and pick one here, and another there, all the time keeping a sharp look out for both pheasant and partridge nests. She used to break a bough in the hedge, where a nest was, and then Harry would go down, guided by the broken bough, and take the eggs. If you came upon her, of course she was only looking for a bird's nest; true, so far, but the nest was a partridge's or pheasant's nest.

When I learned that Master Harry was in the habit of taking our game and eggs, and that he humbugged the magistrates, and defied me, I determined to put a stopper on his little games; he had done Old Dick, but he shouldn't do me. So I kept a sharp look out, and, at the same time, considered the matter carefully, but after a deal of thinking it over the solution of the difficulty came quite by accident.

Keepers if they use a little bait, can make some very useful and sworn 'pals.' Now I had a pal named William Cox, who lived at Amersham Common, and for whom I had, some time previously, done a service which converted him from an enemy into a sworn friend. His home was at the corner of Coppeyson's Lane that led to Weedon Hill Road, and Hyde Heath Common. Well, Cox told me that Harry Wright, the miller, had asked him to look out when he was at work on Mr. Ware's farm for any nests or leverets in the wheat fields. Harry had offered to give him a shilling for each leveret and nest he found. Cox was not to run any risks, all he had to do was to bend down a bough just over every nest he found, and tell Harry whether it was hazel, maple, crab, or hornbeam. So Wright was, afterwards, to go and take the nest, and Cox would have nothing to do with the matter to all appearances.

"Well, mate," said I, after Cox had told me all this. "We can manage for you to get a bob out of him, I think."

"How, so," said Cox.

"Oh, I'll manage that all right if you'll follow my instructions." Cox promised that he would, so I continued:—"Now I know of a pheasant's nest in Odd's Wood, about ten or twelve yards from the common. You say he has made an appointment with you for after breakfast, on Sunday morning, and said:—'all the nests you find tell me of, and I'll pay you for them; you can earn ten shillings or so if you only keep your eyes open.' Is that all Wright said?"

"Yes, and enough, too, ain't it, John?" said Cox, looking up from his work with a grin.

"Now, look you here, Cox," I continued. "You meet me on Saturday night, at the end of Old Beech Lane, and I'll show you the nest I spoke of." This was the Thursday.

"Agreed," said he. "I'll be there at a quarter before eight."

I left him, mightily pleased and much amused, for I may as well mention here that that portion of the wood never contained a single pheasant's nest, the pheasants invariably nesting in the lower woods. Notwithstanding this, I saw, in my mind's eye, a nice little clump of briar, not too thick, and a neatly made nest containing a dozen eggs, underneath. I had not only to make the nest, but also to lay the eggs, myself. Father knew all the nests as well as I did, and was very particular in counting the eggs, so I had to take one here and another there, and then I could only make up four or five, so I made shift for the rest with rotten eggs. Then I put them all into the nest with a good handful of pheasant's feathers, and arranged feathers and eggs to look as much like the real thing as possible, and very real it looked. "Now

Harry, my boy," said I to myself, said I. "If you'll only come to take that nest, with your sweetheart and Harding, you're welcome."

True to his promise Cox met me, on the Saturday night, at Beech Lane, and I took him into Odd's Wood and showed him the nest. He then went outside the wood to the common, and broke a twig in the hedge, leaving it hanging down half broken.

"Now, Cox," said I. "Mind you don't come inside the wood to show him the nest." He grinned, and winked, and left.

The next morning I lay hid near the nest, pretty early, and about eight o'clock Harry and his two help mates arrived with my pal, Cox. When he reached the broken twig, Harry went into the wood alone, made straight for the nest, and collared the eggs in two grabs; then he rejoined his accomplices, Cox having left previously. The three now walked down the common, for about fifty yards, till they came to a gate, in a footpath that led through Odd's Wood, by Hangman's Dell, to Foxe's Mill and Chesham. This footpath cuts the corner of the wood, and leads straight to the place where I was concealed, so I went to meet them.

"Good morning, John," says Harry, as soon as he sees me.

"Good morning, Harry," says I, politely.

"I was just remarking," says Harry, "What a pity it is to cut down such nice, young oak timber, just growing into money." Whereat his two companions burst out laughing, thinking, no doubt, how nicely he was smoothing me over.

"You seem amused, my dear," he went on, pleasantly, addressing the maid, who had a nest full of eggs in her hands. "She is so fond of bird's eggs, John." This to me, of course. They all laughed again at this, and I, nothing loth, joined in. When I thought that they had laughed enough, at my expense, I stepped up to Harry, who was still on the grin, and said:—

"Yes, and so are you fond of bird's eggs, aren't you?"

In a moment his countenance changed, and the grin grew ghastly, as he angrily asked what I meant.

WILKINS SMASHING THE ROTTEN EGGS IN HARRY WRIGHT'S POCKET.

"I mean," said I, "That pocketful of pheasant's eggs you took from that clump of briars up yonder." And before he knew what I was up to, I struck his pockets with the flat of my hand, and smash went the rotten eggs! At this he began cursing and swearing, but I merely remarked:—"Good morning, Harry." Then, turning to the other two, I observed:— "You won't be so fast to laugh at John Wilkins another time, perhaps."

Thereupon I left them, I indulging in a little mirth on my own account, but you should have seen the change that came over their countenances! They had been chuckling to think how nicely Harry was smoothing me down, when they suddenly discovered that I had seen him take the eggs, and saw me convict him before their very eyes. I went home, and told father that I had caught Harry Wright taking a pheasant's nest in Odd's Wood, when he said:—

"Odd's Wood? why I didn't think there was such a thing as a pheasant's nest there."

"No, father," said I. "I daresay not but it's

not far from Beech Wood and one may have strayed up Old Beech Lane to Odd's Wood."

"Yes," replied he, drily. "That must have been it I suppose."

I had a bit of a snack, and then went off again. Some two hours later I met father in Boxhill plantation, and he said:—

"There's a pretty 'to do' about your catching Harry Wright."

"How so?" I asked.

"Why, Mr. Fuller has just been up to me about it, and told me that Harry had visited him."

"Well," said I. "And what of that?"

"He told Mr. Fuller that you had taken him in."

"How?" I asked, assuming surprise.

"He told Mr. Fuller that you had made a nest in Odd's Wood, which some chap told him of, and he was tempted to take it, whilst you were concealed, watching him all the time."

I looked father straight in the face and laughed heartily, saying:—" Another 'sandy rabbit' tale, but it won't wash this time, he should remember that he hasn't got Old Dick to deal with now, and so he'll find out, I can tell you."

"That's just what Mr. Fuller told Harry," said my father, also laughing. "But Harry said that you had made this nest to take him in, and that he could prove it.

"Do so," said Mr. Fuller. So Harry offs with coat, and turned out his pockets, exclaiming:—

"Look, sir, rotten eggs! you see for yourself, sir; pheasants don't lay good and rotten eggs in the same nest."

"No," says Mr. Fuller. "That's quite true, they do not!"

"Well, sir," says Wright. "You see it's a take in, don't you."

"Not a bit of it," says Mr. Fuller. "You keep a lot of fowls, and ducks, and sandy rabbits! it's very easy for you to go straight home, take a rotten egg out of your hen's nest, break it in your pocket, and then come here and show it to me. Just as easy as shooting a tame sandy rabbit, and bringing it before the magistrates, eh, Wright? Another of your dodges! I don't believe a word of your tale."

"But see, sir," says Wright. "Here are the bits of shell belonging to the rotten eggs."

"I don't believe a word you say, Wright," persisted Mr. Fuller. "It's only another of your sandy rabbit tricks. John would not have been so sharp as to put rotten eggs into a nest."

So, off went Mr. Fuller, leaving Harry crestfallen.

Before Mr. Fuller could summon him, Wright sloped off to London and got into the City Police. He could not put up with the neighbours' chaff, such as :—

"How about those rotten eggs, Harry? did young Jack give you a Sunday breakfast off rotten eggs? how did your sweetheart and Harding like the breakfast, Harry?"

So Harry made a bolt of it.

Harding didn't hear the last of it for some time, being often asked how he liked his Sunday treat of rotten eggs that 'young Lukey' treated him to. My real name is John, but father's name being Luke, people often called me 'young Lukey.'

HARRY WRIGHT CAUGHT IN A TRAP. 117

Wright had paid Cox a shilling 'for being trapped,' he said, for he told Mr. Fuller it was a trap, set by me and Cox, to catch him.

"Well," said Mr. Fuller. "Trap or no trap, you are caught, it appears. You've set many traps and now you are caught in one yourself."

Mr. Fuller never asked me whether I had trapped Wright or not, so he did not know if Harry's tale was a 'sandy rabbit' one, for certain. Father always spoke to me as if I had trapped Harry, but I did not want to split on Cox, so never admitted it; if I had, it would have been known that Cox was in the swim with me. Thus it was never clearly understood how Harry had been caught; some thought I trapped him, others believed it to be 'a tale of cock and bull' on Harry's part. Some said it was a shame if I had trapped him, others said it served him Wright (more of my humour) as they had heard him tell me I had not brains enough to catch him, and, if ever I did, he would be the death of me. This was quite true, as I have before related, but I presume he did not mean it, when he said it, since here I am, fifty years after, alive and well.

CHAPTER XII.

THE MONEY COINERS.

I HAVE previously stated that old Dick took a public house, but his first venture as a publican was not such a great success as it might have been, as I will show.

About twelve months after the "rotten eggs" episode, three strangers came prowling around Chesham, Hyde Heath, and the neighbourhood, passing bad money. They did it very cleverly and systematically, and deluged the place with bad half-crowns before they left, which latter operation they deferred rather too long, as I will explain. Amongst others places they

WILKINS AND THE POLICEMAN CHASING THE COINERS.

visited old Dick's pub, and there passed a quantity of bad coins.

One morning, when I was in the yard clearing out the dog kennels, I saw two men on Suthrey's Hill—Mr. Lownde's land—chasing three other men. I knew the two men well; one was Squire Lownde's shepherd, and the other was Sam Smith, the under constable. Sam Smith called out to me, at the same time pointing to the three men who were running away, and off I went, full speed. My father caught sight of me, and shouted, but I pretended not to hear, and kept on. By the time I reached the two men they were breathless, and gaspingly informed me that the three men they were pursuing were those who had been palming off bad money all over the place. They had run them from within a mile of Chesham, up to the Devil's Den Wood.

I joined in the chase, but, as the other two were dead beat, they asked me to stop 'till they recovered their breath. Under the circumstances I thought we had better turn back, and pretend to give up the pursuit as hopeless.

We did so, taking care that the other men should see us walking away from them, as if we did not mean to follow any longer. So they went on towards the Den, whilst we pretended to go back to Chesham.

This ruse succeeded splendidly. I knew every hedge, tree, stick, ditch, lane and path about the place, and being well aware that the men would have to go down a narrow, zigzag lane used as a farm track for carting, I led my companions down a short cut, by a large quickset hedge, to an elbow in the lane. Peeping through the hedge we saw our three gentlemen coming leisurely down the lane, evidently thinking that the pursuit was over. When they were within twenty or thirty yards of us, we all sprang over the hedge. I was told off to spot a man dressed in a pilot coat, and wearing his black curly hair very long, like a girl's. I got up to them in a twinkling, and not troubling about the other two men, who immediately jumped over the hedge, I made for the pilot-coated man. He ran up the lane and I laughed to myself as I gradually overhauled him. Soon, however, I was laughing the wrong side of the mouth, for, stopping a second, he whipped off his slippers or low shoes and then ran from me just like a greyhound. I never saw a man run so fast, he simply flew up the lane to the Devil's Den, as if I were standing still. After he had disappeared and I was standing still staring helplesly at nothing, the shepherd and constable came up. "Well, have you got him? where is he?" they asked. "I should be very much obliged if you could tell me," said I, "for I have clean lost him. But where's your two?" "Oh! they were over the hedge and across the field, before we could look round." Whilst we were talking we spied two of the men, a quarter of a mile away, on the other side of the hill, waiting for the man in the pilot coat, who was walking leisurely up to join them. They all three stood still looking at us, taking off their hats, and beckoning us to come on. We beckoned them to come to us, but they evinced no disposition to do so, and we then gave them a parting salute of a satirical nature, which they returned;

after which we made off in the direction of Chesham.

As soon as we were out of sight of the men, Smith, the constable, and myself turned back again after them; the shepherd, however, left us and went on to Chesham and reported the matter, stating that we were still in pursuit, going towards Ashbridge or Cholsburg Common. This news caused about twelve or fifteen young tradesmen, who had been fleeced by the coiners, to come out and follow in the chase.

We first sighted our men near Ashbridge, or Chartridge Village. Smith and I went into the public house, and there we heard that the three men had just gone by, so I pulled off my heavy keeper's jacket and necktie, to lighten myself as much as possible, preparatory to another chase. Then I put on a sleeve waistcoat, which I borrowed from the landlady, and gave my watch into her keeping.

We then left the public house, and had not got very far out of the village, when I saw all three men going down a footpath leading out of the village, off the high road. This footpath was a right of way, alongside a large, thick-set hedge. I pointed out the men to Smith, and bade him follow me quietly; then I turned down the other side of the hedge. They had not seen us so far, so, running noiselessly down till we got about opposite to them, we then crept along our side of the hedge, until we came to a gate which led through the hedge to the footpath. I jumped over this gate right in front of them, whereupon they immediately made off, I after them.

It had been agreed between Smith and myself that I should not lose another chance by spotting a particular man, but should collar the first one I got near. With me was a blacksmith, who had joined us, and Smith was close behind with the darbies. I collared the first man, and Smith handcuffed him, after which I gave chase to the others. By this time, however, they had poached a good start, but I had not run many hundred yards before I reached the pilot-coated man. He begged, he cried, he fell on his knees, and entreated me to let him go. Up came Smith with his prisoner, and secured the 'Flying Dutchman' as I facetiously dubbed the man with pilot-coat. "Go on Jack," roared Smith excitedly, "Let's have all three, and make a job of it. We'll be after you."

Off I went after the third man, who was a horse dealer, and very strong and tall. He had about two hundred yards' start and was running well, so that I had to run quite six hundred yards before I caught up to him; then I pinned him up in a corner close to a wood. He had a large crab stick, a twitchel used for holding horses, in one hand, and a stone in the other, and he pleasantly swore that he would smash my teeth with his stick, and split my skull with the stone. He emphasized his remarks by a series of prods with the stick, by which means he kept me off. I had no weapon of any kind, but I kept him there for some time, hoping, every moment, that Smith would arrive, but 'nary a Smith appeared. Now, as this man stood about five feet eleven, and weighed about fifteen stone, and was well armed, and as, moreover, I then weighed only a little over eight stone, and was not armed at all, he got away before help came, and I had nothing for it but to hark back. I soon met with Smith, and a farmer named Clare, who was on horseback, and we all three returned to the wood, which we carefully searched. We failed to find anything, and so went back to the public house where I had left my things. It seemed that, after I had started in pursuit of the third man, Smith took his prisoners back towards the public house. Meeting Mr. Clare on the way he explained matters to him, and the latter then ordered his men to take charge of the coiners whilst he himself went with Smith to my assistance.

When we reached the public house we found there a lot of young tradesmen, who had turned out in pursuit of the coiners, as I have before mentioned. They were very mighty in their conversation, saying what they would have done, or would do; what they actually did was—nothing. I never found gas of much use in a row; very few gassy men show up well in a rough and tumble. These young tradesmen, however, had all been cheated by the coiners.

After partaking of refreshment we all set out for Chesham. Some of the shopkeepers wanted Smith to take the darbies off the 'Flying Dutchman,' give him twenty yards start, and let him race me. Smith declined, sententiously observing that they'd already had enough trouble to catch them, and, being a constable, there was nothing in his indentures that warranted him in releasing a prisoner, before handing him over to the proper authorities. So we marched into Chesham with two out of the three coiners. The town was all up in arms; it was like a fair. Nearly every shopman came out to his door to greet us, and some offered us drink, and some gave us money; every one was wild with excitement over our capture.

After seeing the coiners safely in the lock-up, we all agreed to go up to old Dick's place, and spend the day playing skittles. As we were passing by the Queen's Head, the last public house in Chesham, out ran Harry Wright, and says he:—"Come in and have a glass, Jack;

you've put six or seven shillings in my pocket, already, this morning. I was told that Lukey had gone after those chaps. 'Is it young or old Lukey,' says I. 'Young Lukey,' says they. 'Then' says I, 'I'll bet a sovereign they'll bring back two out of the three; young Lukey runs like a hare, and springs like a tiger, there's no getting away from him. He'll catch two out of the three, and so you have, Jack, and here's my hand, old man; and we'll forget old scores, and wipe every thing off with a glass of grog."

Then we all turned into the Queen's Head for a few minutes, and Harry and I wiped out all ill-feeling, over a glass. He told me he was getting on very well in the police, and had just run down for a few days' holiday.

After this we went off to old Dick's, to tell him the news, for these three men had played " Jack's alive " at his house pretty frequently. Every time they went there they had called for beer, and tendered a half-crown in payment, so that poor old Dick had a good store of bad coins. As we passed our house, father came out and called me aside. He asked me not to go on with the rest, as he said they were up for a spree. " Besides,". he added, " Harry Wright is with them, and he might think about the rotten eggs job, you know, John."

"Oh, he's all right with me now father," said I. "We've made all that up over a glass at the Queen's Head." "Ay ay," persisted my father, "That may be very well, but Harry's a quarrelsome fellow, and when the wine's in, the wit's out; so don't you go, John."

Much against my inclinations, I determined to take my father's advice, so, going out to the others, I made some sort of excuse to get out of it. I said that Mr. Fuller wanted me, or something of that sort, and they left, on my making a half promise that I would look them up later on. I did not do this, and, curiously enough, I have never since seen Harry Wright from that day to this.

The third coiner was soon 'nobbled,' and the three were sent to Aylesbury for trial. Smith, Lovering, myself, and others gave evidence against them, and they were convicted; the horse dealer man got six months ' and hard,' the other two, four months each. These latter laid all the blame on their companion; they both said that he had sent them into shops to buy small-priced things, such as an ounce of tobacco, and had given them these half crowns to pay with, they not knowing that the money was bad. They were all three strangers to each other, so they said, and on the tramp in search of work. The pilot-coated man said that he was a journeyman-blacksmith on his way to London, that he fell in with the horse dealer and his van, and that they then made an agreement whereby the former was to assist him with his van and horses, the horse dealer, in return, providing board and lodging, free of cost. He knew nothing of the bad money, but, in cross-examination, admitted having suspicions about it, because of the changing it at so many places.

I was in court the whole time, and paid strict attention to the evidence, and at first, I thought that there was just a possibility that these two men had been taken in by the horse dealer. But undoubtedly they found him out after awhile, and still continued to pass the money for him, probably sharing the proceeds, so that they were really just as bad as he. Birds of a feather flock together, and I would have punished them more severely if possible.

CHAPTER XIII.

OF ALEXANDER.

AFTER the capture of the coiners, as Wright was done for, we had no more trouble with poachers for some time. The defeat of Wright, who was a ruling spirit amongst these gentry, seemed to have discouraged them. So I only remained under-keeper to Mr. Fuller for a short time, as I was offered a berth as head-keeper to General Popham, at Littlecote, Chilton House, Chilton Ffolliot, Wilts; I took it. Afterwards I went as keeper for the Rev. Henry Fowle, of Chute Lodge, near Andover, Hants. This was in the year 1840, and his father and mother were living at Chute Lodge then, but they both soon died, and after that I went back again to Chilton House. A Major Symons had taken it, and the shooting attached. Whilst I was there I caught some nine or ten poachers, but I will only relate the circumstances of one capture, as it began in a rather desperate affray, and ended in a ludicrous one. (*Ex uno disce omnes.—Eds.*)

An oldish man, of the name of Alexander, lived at Littlecote; he was a confirmed poacher both of game and fish, and as cunning as they make 'em. He was most daring too, and nobody could catch him, although he had often been known to visit his snares and traps in open day, under a keeper's very nose, and yet had not been nobbled. All this Tom Pounds, the General's river and fish keeper, told me, adding that Alexander was also very strong and determined.

All my life, I have only gone one way to work to catch poachers, and I believe it is the only safe way; I always do all the watching myself, and never entrust it to anyone else. It is of no use to trust to anything you hear about an infallible method of catching poachers in all countries. Where poaching has been extensively and successfully carried on, the keepers have no one to thank for it but themselves. When keepers fall into a slack way of doing their duties, either through wilful neglect or incapacity, all the idle hands in the neighbourhood soon get to know it, and poaching, which always offers strong temptations to the idle and lazy, is carried on with more or less success; then, when a new keeper comes on the scene, and finds such a state of affairs, his position is not an agreeable one.

Before I had been at Chilton House a week I discovered the old signs, a hedge set with snares, in a small spring called Oaken Copse. I watched these snares all day, in company with Tom Pounds, and at last he said:—"I think they've got wind as there's a new keeper on, and that's why they won't come. Suppose you go into Ramsbury and have half a pint of beer; take care to show yourself as you walk away, and remain for an hour or so, whilst I stop here and watch. If they see you going off, on the road to Ramsbury, they'll think that now is their chance, and so I shall catch them."

Pounds thought that these snares were set by Alexander, and, as he seemed most anxious to catch him, I did as he suggested. Alexander had, it seemed, caused Tom a lot of trouble by laying night lines for trout in the streams.

When I had gone, a heavy shower of rain came on, which caused Pounds to leave his hiding place and take shelter behind some large trees further in the copse. After the storm had passed he went back to the snares, and found them gone.

Tom Pounds told me, on my return, that the poacher had come and removed the snares during the storm. We agreed to meet at the same place early next morning, and then Pounds left.

When he had gone I walked across to the hedge, as I suspected he had been played an old poaching trick. It turned out that he had, for I found that the snares had not been removed altogether; they had merely been run down and concealed in the grass, ready for re-setting at a moment's notice. "Ah!" said I to myself, "I think I'll assist at the next setting of this lot."

This is a common trick with poachers, and often takes in a keeper who is not up to his work. A snaring poacher invariably sets his snares in as secret a way as possible, and always in the best hedgerows for taking; he finds these out by observation when he is at work in the fields. A hare or rabbit will always take the same run through a hedge, or into a wood; out of innumerable small runs it will invariably choose its own main run. It is a wonderful thing, but each run or road is exclusively the property of the family who first made it. When a hare or rabbit is 'started' it makes for its own run, and if driven by fear into one that does not belong to it, the effect is at once shown by a marked decrease in speed. A labourer at work in a field observes this, and can swear to the particular point at which a hare or rabbit, started from any given part of the field, will enter a wood, even if that wood be half a mile off. But I digress.

The snares, as I have before remarked, had been 'run down.' Instead of being set, they had been taken out of the split stick, and run out of the loop, the whole wire being then hidden in the long grass. A wire can be easily concealed, but, if a snare is pulled up, there is bound to be a mess, which soon attracts the eye. Pounds was to meet me next morning at Oaken Copse, and not before, so I lighted my pipe and sauntered out into the open, where I could be easily seen by anyone on the watch. After hanging about for half an hour or so, I deliberately turned my back on the copse, and went off in the opposite direction. I had made up my mind to follow my old methods, and, if possible, to catch the poacher red handed; so I thought I would give him every opportunity of resetting the snares, and this is why I pretended to go away. In case anyone was watching me, he would conclude that the snares had not been discovered, as they were not taken up, and my reasoning proved correct, for, on arriving there early next morning, I found the snares all reset.

Pounds did not turn up, nor did anyone else, but I watched them all day until dusk, when, it being Sunday, I knocked off, intending to return before daybreak next morning.

When I arrived next morning it was, of course, dark, but I just managed to make out something in one of the snares, which afterwards turned out to be a leveret, still alive, about the size of a full grown rabbit. I had been watching only a little while, and day was beginning to break, when I saw a man creep through the hedge and proceed to examine the snares. When he discovered the leveret he glanced cautiously all around, then removed it from the wire still alive, and put it in his pocket. The animal gave a kick, and jumped out of one side of his smock frock, but, being half dead, it travelled slowly, so he fell on his hands and knees and crawled after it. Before he could reach it, I sprang forward, and caught him by the collar, the leveret escaping.

We had a sharp tussle for some time; he

managed to get up off the ground, and as I held him with my left hand only, he got hold of my gun, which I held in my right. Seizing the stock with one hand and the barrel with the other, he gave a twist and wrenched it away from me. Letting go of his collar, I immediately seized the gun and we struggled together to obtain possession of it; sometimes he got it away from me for a few seconds, and then I would recapture it again, and had it all to myself for a while; then we both had hold of it, and so the fight went on until at last I got it fairly away from him, when he ran at me to knock me down, I struck out at him with my gun, aiming at his head, but he put up his hand and warded off the blow; then clenching both hands round the weapon he backed me against a stub, which manœuvre had the effect of nearly upsetting me. Seeing me totter he made a rush at me to pin me down, so I clubbed my weapon, and struck at him with the butt end. He dodged the blow and caught hold of the butt, so that I was left half on the ground, clutching the barrels, and as these were wet and slippery he soon got the gun away from me.

We had now been at it about ten minutes, and were both pretty well blown, still I had plenty of fight in me. I sprang to my feet and seeing that he was feeling for a knife, kept on twisting him round so that he could not get at it. I had nothing to defend myself, or attack him with now, and as fast as I approached him he kept prodding me with the gun barrel, and kicking at me. Cocking the gun, he shouted to me to stand off or he'd be the death of me, but, luckily, in the struggle amongst the brush wood, both caps had fallen off the nipples, so I escaped unhurt. Finding this, he clubbed the gun and threatened to smash my brains out. I was very much nettled, for although I could see that he hadn't much more fight left in him, he had the gun, so what could I do? He was much bigger and stronger than I, and weighed I should say, over fourteen stone, whilst I only weighed between eight and nine stone; but what I lacked in strength and weight I made up for in youth and toughness, for he must have been considerably over forty at the time. I, therefore, had to leave him in possession of the field, with my gun, I having no weapon available, not even a stone; had there been any handy I believe I should have used them, sooner than be beaten. I told him this and that I knew his name was Alexander, and so, reluctantly, departed, going right up into the wood.

After a few minutes I met a man called Hobbs, who was just beginning his work of hedging; I told him the story and he returned with me to the scene of my late encounter, taking with him a stout sapling. Alexander was gone, but Hobbs found my gun about twenty yards away from the place where we had fought.

Alexander absconded, but a warrant was issued, and five pounds reward was offered for his apprehension, and he was taken, about five or six months afterwards, on the rail-road at Swindon. He was brought to Chilton, and sent to Marlborough for trial. He was charged with " attempting to kill or do some grievous bodily harm." He employed Counsel to defend him, and this Counsel was a very smart man; I myself saw and heard him get two men off for stealing corn out of an allotment ground, and also two men who had stolen some cheese. All these cases were as clear as the daylight, and it was only through the slovenly police evidence, and the smartness of the defending lawyer, that the accused men got off. On the strength of these cases Alexander employed this Counsel, whose name was Ball.

When our case came on all the witnesses were ordered out of court. I was called first, and when I stood in the witness box, Mr. Ball was just at my side, and before he began to cross-examine me, he stuck an eyeglass, about the size of a policeman's bull's-eye, in his eye. Then he took it down, and then put it up again, and so on; every time he put up his eyeglass he settled his tie and gave vent to an expressive :— "Ahem!" After he had been playing these games some little time I thought I would follow suit, so I "speered" up to him and ruffling up my hair with my right hand—which was another favourite trick of his—I remarked:—" Ahem!' just as I had heard him do. Hereupon everyone in court burst out laughing, judge and jury with the rest, and some one called out:—" The little bantam against the old turkey cock."

Counsellor Ball was a big heavy man of fifteen or sixteen stone, whereas I am very short and light, so, as compared with him, I must have looked very much like a bantam cock, in point of size. I may add that I felt very much like that bird, for I never could stand bullying of any kind.

Well, after silence was restored, I was ordered to state the case. Now I never could relate the simplest thing without a certain amount of acting. In my opinion, if a story is worth telling at all it is worth telling properly, and a little acting should therefore be introduced into it. So I had not been in the witness box two minutes before I was carried away with the thoughts of my recent struggle, and lived over again, in imagination, every single incident of that adventure. I was on my hands and knees in the court, and a police officer to impersonate Alexander. Then I was supplied with a stick to take the place of the gun, and so went to work.

I put the policeman in the exact position of Alexander, on his hands and knees, with his back towards me, as if taking the leveret out of the snare. Then I crept up behind him, with the stick in my left hand, and seized him by the collar.

I should mention here that this police officer was a very intelligent young man, and, having listened attentively to my account of the fray, he entered into the spirit of the thing most heartily. The moment my hand was on his collar he rounded on me, and caught hold of the stick. I instantly forgot all about acting, the court, and everything else; all I knew was that I had met a man of my own calibre. At it we went, up and down the place, for about five minutes, the whole court roaring with laughter. Robert was an active young man, and gave me quite as much trouble as Alexander had done. How it might have ended I do not know, for first he got the stick, and then I did and so it went on, until something happened which brought our pantomime to a premature close.

Whether it had been placed there purposely or not I can't say, but, about the spot where I had said the alder stump would be, was a low gangway, board, or partition, not much higher than one's knee. In our last rally, when I had fairly got the gun to myself, my antagonist backed me up against this door; feeling myself going, I loosed hold of the stick suddenly. The effect was that I tumbled head over heels over the partition squash into a couple of fat, old Counsellors, who were vigorously taking notes. I fell head downwards, and, the board being so low, my legs were left sticking up in the air, whilst the court house rang with uproarious laughter.

As soon as I extricated myself the ushers were calling "silence," and, on order being restored, Counsellor Ball began his speech for the defence. He contended that it was only a case of common assault, as Alexander was an utter stranger to me, and I to him; therefore, when a man, armed with a gun came up, and did not announce himself as a gamekeeper, he (Alexander) naturally thought it was with an intention to shoot or rob him. Such being the case, it was naturally Alexander's first move to try and possess himself of the gun, and so preserve his life. Again, he said it was I who began the assault, and he laid special stress on the fact that I had not said anything about being a gamekeeper, contending that it would have most materially altered the case if we had known each other.

The trial lasted four hours and forty minutes, and the jury found Alexander guilty of assault only; he was sentenced to two years' imprisonment in the new county goal at Devizes. "Thank you, my Lord," said he when he heard the sentence, "I shall know where to hang up my hat there." I understood this remark when they told me that he had eaten thirteen Christmas dinners in gaol.

He served his two years, and I heard that he went to gaol again, before he could even reach his home at Ramsbury. Wonderful to relate, after this last dose of gaol he turned over a new leaf, and became an honest, and even a pious and good man. His father, curiously enough, was a Methodist preacher, whom I often used to hear preaching by the road side, at Chilton.

Mr. Ball cross examined me pretty sharply at the trial, but I answered him up, and I think he got almost as good as he gave. There was no doubt in my own mind, that if the caps had not fallen off the gun during the struggle, I should either have been killed or else badly wounded, as there is no knowing what a man will do when his blood is up. I never bore malice, though, and if Alexander did snap the gun at me, I am quite willing to put it down as an accident, though, had the caps been on, the probability is that I should never have written this book.

After the trial I met the policeman who had impersonated Alexander, outside the court, and complimented him on his acting, telling him that if he had been Alexander himself, and actually fighting for the gun, he could not have done it better. We had a friendly glass of beer together, and I told him that if ever he got tired of the force there was always a good opening for him as a gamekeeper.

I heard afterwards that he had stuck to the force, and had been well promoted, but I have lost sight of him for so long now that I don't know whether he is still living or not.

END OF BOOK I.

BOOK II.

CHAPTER I.

CONCERNING DOGS.

HITHERTO I have confined my remarks to reminiscences of my youthful life as a keeper, just jotting down events as they from time to time occur to my mind; but now I have had a gentle reminder from my biographer to the following effect :—" Look here, Wilkins, these anecdotes are all very well, but if you want your book to go down with the public, you must not only make it interesting, but also instructive."

Now, when an old man like myself is set down to write his life and adventures, he must be allowed to write it in his own way; whether my way is interesting and instructive I don't know, but I do know that I never bargained for all this writing, and, if ever it appears in print before the public, they must take it for what it is worth. I am going to devote this chapter to dogs—sporting dogs, and the very words I wanted are put into my mouth—'interesting,' and 'instructive.'

Many keepers will tell you that there are several different methods of breaking in dogs, I myself have seen various methods tried, and have come to the conclusion that there is only one which can be successfully adopted for all dogs, and that is kindness, patience, and perseverance. Interest your young dog, whilst you are instructing him.

I intend to deal with three kinds of dogs—setters, pointers, and retrievers, but the same rules to be observed in breaking these dogs can (with very slight alterations) be applied to all other dogs, according to what they are required for.

I broke my first brace of young pointers for

the Rev. Mr. Fowle, at Chilton. My father shortly afterwards came down to Chilton, and saw these young dogs out at work. He told Mr. Fuller, when he got home, that he was amazed at my dogs, and quite ashamed of himself for having, some time previously, kicked me out of the field with a smack of the ear, telling me I had not got the brains of a sprat for dog-breaking, and he should never be able to make anything of me. Not only he, but many other people, found out their mistake in this special branch of a keeper's duty, for they discovered, as I shall explain, that to thrash a young dog is to spoil him, and that scores of valuable dogs have been destroyed as useless, simply because of faults that were instilled into them by gross ignorance and mismanagement.

In the year 1843, I came to Stanstead, Essex, as gamekeeper to William Fuller-Maitland Esquire, and there I have remained ever since. After I had been there two years, Mr. Fuller was down shooting at Ereswell, near Mildon Hall, Suffolk, and, on his way back to Chesham, he called at Stanstead to shoot with Mr.

Fuller-Maitland for a week. On his return to Chesham, Mr. Fuller sent for my father, and in the course of conversation, said:—"I have been shooting with your son's master, at Stanstead." Then my father asked how I was getting on, and received a favourable reply. Then said my father, with a twinkle in his eye:—"Well sir, there is one thing I should like to ask you; did you see any of the dogs he has broken?" "Yes, I did," said Mr. Fuller. "And what did you think of them, sir?" "You shall know what I think, Luke," replied Mr. Fuller. "You shall never break another dog, for me or anyone else, so long as you are in my service; if ever I want another dog broken, I shall send it to your son John, at Stanstead."

So he did, and father never broke another dog from that time to the day of his death. I, alone, broke Mr. Fuller's pointers and setters, until he died; George Rose, underkeeper to Mr. Fuller, may have broken a few retrievers fo him, but I don't think he did.

In breaking dogs, the first thing to be considered is the age. It is a difficult, and almost useless job to attempt to break a dog who has passed his youth, and is well into his second year; dogs who are worth breaking, should be taken in hand when from eight to twelve months old.

Let the young dog hunt at liberty over land where larks and partridges are plentiful, he will then first begin to hunt the larks, next turning his attention to the partridges, and, after this, he will know that he is hunting for game, and will chase the birds with delight.

Next he must be taught to 'drop to the hand,' and for this you must make the following preparations. Drive a stiff peg, about the stoutness of a fold-stake, into the ground, leaving from eight to twelve inches exposed. Then take a strong cord about twenty yards long, fasten one end to the peg, and the other to the dog's neck, so that he cannot slip it over his head, but not so as to let it 'jam' or you will throttle your dog. Now take your dog up to the peg and tell him to 'down,' at the same time putting him flat on the ground, but he will not stay down for a moment after your eye is off him.

After telling him authoritatively to 'down,' start off running away from him. Immediately, disobeying his orders the dog gets up and runs after you, but when he gets to the end of the cord, it will throw him head over heels backwards. You should run as fast as ever you can because, the sharper the fall the dog gets, the more careful he becomes, and the sooner he learns the lesson you wish to teach him.

Directly the dog is thrown backwards, turn about, pull him back to the peg, and tell him to 'down,' holding up your hand as before. You will have to repeat the experiment of running away from him, again and again, for before the dog can be made to understand he will have had at least a dozen nasty falls. Every time you should pull him back to the peg again, talking seriously to him, and calling 'down,' at the same time holding up your hand. Don't slur your part of the work, as it is most essential that the word of command should be accompanied by the action of the hand; after a time the dog's attention being fixed upon you, the action of the hand will be sufficient without

DOG BREAKING. WILKINS SPEAKING SERIOUSLY TO THE DOG.

saying anything, as the dog will know what is meant, but in 'breaking, both must be given. I have frequently called dogs by their names, two or three hundred yards off, holding up my hand, when they drop immediately.

When at last you get the dog to lay quiet at the peg, run away from him, run past him, and walk round him, for a quarter of an hour on end. If, during this time, he attempts to get up, put him down as before, holding up your hand and saying 'down,' and, by this means, he will soon learn to lay quiet at the peg After he will do this, you should pat him and encourage him, telling him to get up; if he is a nervous or timid dog you had better not try him any more that day, but if he does not seem to care or be alarmed, go on with the practice forthwith. You must use your own judgment in this matter.

The completion of the peg practice consists in making him 'drop' at any given length of the cord, from the peg to the extreme length. Walk the dog round and round the peg so as to shorten the length of the cord, then set off running past the peg, until you come nearly to the end of the cord, and, just as he feels it tightening, stop short, calling out 'down' and holding up your hand. Be careful not to throw the dog, as if he obeys you at once, it gives him confidence, whereas, if he is thrown, he does not know whether it is his fault or not. Keep him at this practice for three or four days, until he will lay quiet at the peg, or at any intermediate distance between it and the end of the cord.

The next thing is the practice with the forty yards cord. Put a small cord, about forty yards long, round the neck of the dog, and hold the other end in your hand all the time, watching for a favourable opportunity to cry 'down' and hold up your hand; this should be done, if possible, when the dog is coming straight at you. Now one of two things will take place— the dog will either drop obediently, or he will bolt straight for home. If the former happens, well and good, he has profited by instruction; if the latter happens, take care to give him a smart fall when he gets to the end of his tether, then pull him back to the exact place where you required him to 'down,' force him down there, and then resume your original position, making him lay there and assume the precise position he wished to shirk. Keep him there, as in the peg practice, whilst you walk round and round him for some time; then resume the practice, until you can trust him to drop at forty yards with certainty.

When this has been accomplished, you may let him run with the cord for a while, holding up your hand and crying 'down,' at intervals; this should be continued until he will drop, at any distance, on your merely holding up your hand without speaking.

After you are thoroughly satisfied that the dog has learned obedience to command, both by voice and hand, the next thing is to hunt him with a trained dog. You should always make dogs lay at the 'down,' until you go to them and tell them to get up; this is most essential, as by accustoming dogs to be raised by the word of command only, they will keep at the 'down' until such word be given.

When you have put the dog you are training with a dog already trained, keep on dropping them alternately, until the former has learned not to rise until he is told to. An intelligent dog soon observes what his companion does, and imitates it. At first there may be a little difficulty in keeping your untrained dog at 'the down,' when he sees the other dog hunting; but when he is raised himself, and sees the other at 'the down,' he soon learns not to rise unless ordered by word of command.

The word of command to raise dogs should simply be the calling out of their names, and as you walk towards your dog, wave your hand gently, as if encouraging him to get up and hunt.

You should keep the dogs hunting round each other, taking care not to let them get too far away. I have done this practice with thirteen dogs at a time, keeping the whole lot at 'the down' for a while, and then raising one here, and another there, allowing no dog to stir unless ordered to, until I have gradually raised twelve out of the thirteen, all of whom then hunted round the one dog still at 'the down'

After you have taught your dog to drop at any distance, you may take him into the field to learn the further duties for which he has been bred, and from whence he derives his name—to 'point,' or 'set' as the case may be. Hitherto your labour has been directed towards teaching your dog obedience to the word of command, and your practices have therefore taken place in those spots which were most convenient to yourself, but the reality of a dog's life begins when he is taken into the field.

The natural instinct of these dogs is to point, or set, but they have to be trained to take the field properly, and be steady in their work. For this reason it is particularly necessary that the day and field should both be well chosen, as on these two circumstances will chiefly depend the success of the remainder of the practices that a pointer or setter, before he can be pronounced thoroughly broken to gun and birds, must undergo. The morning should be bright and fine, so that the birds will 'lay,' and the field should be rather small. Take the dog in, right for the wind, and don't let him get too far away from you. Keep a sharp look out to see when he winds the birds, and, directly he does so, step up to him as quickly as you can, getting your hand ready for the word 'down'; then, if the birds rise, keep him down for a while as at the peg, walk round him, go a little distance away, and fire a pistol, half charged only, so as not to alarm him or make him 'gun-shy,' then go and pat him up, calling him a good dog, and bestowing other canine compliments upon him. Off he goes again, and winds another pair of birds lying in the young wheat or early sown barley, which is tall enough to hide them; then do just the same as before; drop him at the 'down,' fire the pistol, and raise him. You should hunt one dog only at this stage of the training, it is impossible to manage more, as one will take up all your attention.

The next thing is to prevent him from putting his birds up, to teach him to set or point at them only. Let him hunt on for another pair of birds,—so, he has got them again, and is making straight at them, "Down Rollo."

Drop him before he puts up his birds, then walk quietly on and put up the birds yourself, firing the pistol and keeping him 'down' as before. Continue this practice until he learns to drop to his birds. Should he drop to his birds instead of 'pointing' them, you should go very quietly and raise him up, saying :—"Steady, Rollo, at them, good dog, steady, steady," then directly the birds rise :—" Down, Rollo, down, good dog." Walk away, and fire your pistol from a distance as before.

It is of vital importance that the pistol should be fired at a distance, for if a gun is unexpectedly fired over a dog's head you will very likely make him 'gun-shy'; it is far less likely to alarm him when fired some way off and in full view of him, for then he is in some degree prepared for the report. For young dogs, when breaking, I invariably use a pistol half charged, until they become accustomed to the report, then a pistol full charged, and lastly a gun.

Most dogs that are 'gun-shy' are made so by firing the gun over their heads when all their attention is taken up by the scent, and 'pointing' the birds. For instance, we will suppose that a young dog has a staunch 'point' at his birds; two gentlemen walk up towards him, and, when they have got within ten yards or so, a covey of birds rise. Bang, bang, go their guns, just over the animal's head, and away he runs, trembling, and frightened out of his wits. Nothing will now induce him to come up to you, or do any more work, he slinks after you, a field behind, for the rest of the day. I have seen this happen more than once, and almost for a certainty that dog is spoilt, through no fault of his own; many a time a dog is made 'gun-shy' and called a cur, through mismanagement of this kind. Put yourself in the dog's place; you could not stand four or five guns banging off unexpectedly over your head, when your attention was firmly fixed elsewhere, the noise would sound all day in your ears, and you would be either deaf or half crazy.

When a dog is once made gun-shy in the way I have described, the only remedy is to hunt him with a lot of rabbit dogs; in chasing the rabbits with the other dogs in full cry, he will get accustomed to the report of a gun, and will probably recover from his shyness, but he will never be quite the same dog as he would have been had he never been gun-shy. Moreover, he will always be more or less inclined to chase hares, after having been allowed to run in cover with a lot of rabbit dogs.

The next thing to teach the dog is "quartering the land." Take the dog into a field, giving him the wind,—the field should be as narrow as possible so that he may not get away more than fifty or sixty yards on the right or left—blow a whistle to call his attention, then throw your hand from right to left if you want the dog to cross to the left, if to the right, move your hand from left to right. Should he not quarter to the right according to your instructions, but make off straight up the field, you must shout to him to drop. It will most likely be necessary to use a small cord fifty or sixty yards long, you then cross the field holding the end of the cord in your hand, if he still goes off straight give him the whistle, and throw your hand against the land, at the same time walking in that direction and pulling the cord, so as to guide him.

When your dog is at the peg practice, before commencing to hunt him in the field, it is a very good plan to take a live wild rabbit, and turn down before him when at the peg, in order to teach him not to run ground game. To prepare for this you want a piece of cord, fifty or sixty yards long, and a board about six inches square; bore a hole through the centre of the board, put one end of the cord through and secure it by tyiug a knot larger than the hole, the other end of the cord you tie round the rabbit's neck, making a knot so that it shall not choke him. Now turn the rabbit down and let it run by your dog, at the same time calling out to him to 'down'; run after the rabbit, catch it, and put it in your pocket out of the dog's sight. Repeat this again and again in the grove or park, so as to prepare your dog for the field, and then, when the first hare gets up in the field, you will be able to drop him as you did at the peg with the wild rabbit.

This method of teaching a dog is much better than whipping his skin off his ribs. I never use a whip, or even take one with me, when breaking young dogs; some men teach by the whip, but I never knew any good come of using a whip unnecessarily to a young dog, he is invariably cowed or made sulky, and, however good his breed, will never be such a good dog in the field as he would have been had he been taught by kindness and with patience. I say, therefore, to all who wish to break dogs properly:—"Leave the whip at home." Great patience is required in dog breaking, and, if a man be not blessed with that commodity, he had better not attempt to break any dog. Let the young dog punish himself with the cord, throwing himself over by it; two or three wrenching cracks at the neck, caused by his running in when he had no business to, soon makes a dog think and understand, and a lesson once properly understood is soon learnt and never forgotten.

After a young dog is properly broken take a whip out with you, but be careful how you use it, as a young dog will often make mistakes, or be unsteady and run in at the wrong time, through earnestness, or jealousy of another dog. If you perceive this, call the dog to you, and talk to him quietly, cautioning him before you use the whip. With old dogs who know their work, and wilfully transgress and set me at defiance, I do use the whip, perhaps more sharply than most men. The dog has defied me, and it remains to be proved which is master, he or I, and he will have to submit to me before I leave off. One thing I always do after the dog has submitted to me, I make him come and humble himself, lick my hands and so forth, so that we may part good friends. This is a great point with dogs, because, if you let them leave you as soon as you have done thrashing them, they will probably come out on bad terms with you the next day, and remain so for some time.

Never take your dogs into the kennel in a bad temper, cheer them up into a good one, play with them, or give them something nice to eat out of your pocket. You should always carry something, the leg bone of a fowl or anything of that sort, to give them as a prize for doing well, or to get them in a good temper after chastising them; but you must guard against too much of this prize giving, for if you make a practice of it the dog will be continually looking out for it.

In thrashing an old dog who has set you at defiance, it is well to put on a muzzle first, as it enables you to conquer him with about one quarter the thrashing that it would otherwise take; he knows he can't fight, and is therefore beaten, so all he can do is to take as much as you like to give him.

When your young dog is broken, in the manner I have already described, it is necessary to teach him to back other dogs. Take an old dog out with the young one and, when the former gets the point, 'drop' the latter 'till you walk up to the old dog and put up your birds. After dropping him a few times in this way, you should speak to him, holding up your hand and saying:—"Steady, Shot, steady, at them, good dog." If he does not point properly drop him to your hand, and, if he is not inclined to 'back,' take him out alone next morning, and so hunt him for a couple of hours. Then fetch out the old dog and hunt them both together, when the young one, being tired, will more readily back the other.

After he has been at this practice long enough to learn thoroughly to back' with the old dog, leave the latter at home, and take out two young dogs to back each other. Whilst this practice is going on, you should hunt your dog, occasionally, with three or four yards of cord on him; it is useful to take hold of to stop him, running when another dog is on the point, and is also a useful check to prevent him getting away. This finishes the practice for pointers and setters.

CHAPTER II.

INASMUCH AS TO RETRIEVERS.

No retriever puppy ought to be beaten under any circumstances, if you want him to become a good, loving, and obedient companion, and to defend and guard you night and day; by rash treatment you will probably entirely take away his love and repect for you.

"What," say you. "Do you mean to tell me, Wilkins, that a dog has *love* and *respect* for his master"? Yes, yes, yes! I do tell you so most emphatically, and if there is one dog more than another that is possesed of these faculties it is the retriever, and next to him comes the Scotch Collie.

"Well," you may ask, "How are you going to manage a young retriever, without putting your stick across his ribs when he won't obey you?" For one thing, my friend, if you can't manage him without that you can't manage him with it, that's quite certain; he will never be made what a good retriever should be by laying your stick across his ribs when he is a puppy. That may be necessary after he is full grown, sometimes, if he wilfully disobeys you and sets you at defiance; when you do, it is better to give him five or six sharp strokes than to thrash him for an hour, but you should always beat him until he submits, whether it be a matter of five strokes or five and twenty. The moment he does submit throw down your stick and talk very seriously to him for five minutes, until he begs pardon and licks your hand, then pat him up kindly, and he will tell you he is really very sorry for what he did.

This is a very important crisis for both you and the dog, for on his behaviour after his first thrashing, and your own towards him, will chiefly depend what sort of a dog he turns out. When he tells you, as plainly as any dog can, that he is truly sorry for what he has done, you should make friends with him at once, and let him know that you are fond of him notwithstanding the little misunderstanding. It is most essential that you should make, and part, friends.

We will suppose your dog to be five or four months old when you should have him in the house, if your wife does not object, for she can teach him a great deal. It is better still to have him in the house when he is two months old; if your wife objects, you may smooth her over by promising her that, if she will help you to make a good dog of him, and he fetches a good price, she shall have half of it. Be sure to carry out your promise, and then the next time you bring a pup home she will welcome him, knowing it to be to her own pecuniary interest to do so. Your wife will teach the youngster more in the house than you can do—to be clean and obedient, go out and in with her, and learn all she says to him, thus helping you very much in making him a sensible dog. Then, when you come home to meals, you can teach him to fetch and carry things, such things as a ball or anything soft you may have handy to throw for him.

I had a puppy once that would fetch my slippers for me, as soon as he saw me pull my gaiters off and begin unlacing my boots off he'd go across the room for my slippers, and they were by my side before I had time to draw off my boots. Then he would drag my boots off to where I was accustomed to place them, and the gaiters as well, and then he would come up to me, wagging his tail, and lick my hand as if well pleased with his job. Now this is all perfectly true, and not a 'dog' story in the usual sense of the word.

He will get very much attached to your wife —you needn't be jealous—being very glad to go out with her, and will soon learn to obey her, for she can do more towards teaching him obedience than you can. When a piece of meat or bread is left on the table or anywhere about, she will teach him not to touch it without permission. She can teach them a great deal in feeding them, especially if she has two pups, or one pup and another kind of dog, such as a French poodle; she will cut their meat into small pieces like lumps of sugar, and taking one piece at a time, will tell them who it is for. "This is for Topsy. That's for Help, I told you to wait till your turn came, sir." So each dog learns not to touch the other's pieces of meat, and if he does he gets a rap over the head with the handle of a knife.

In this way a puppy gets to know all you say to him, and my wife has been obliged, before now, to spell things out to me, so that the dog should not hear, if we did not want him to go down to the village. If my wife said:—"I am going to Stanstead after dinner, do you want anything?" I might reply:—"Yes, you can get me some tobacco, and you may as well take the dogs with you." The dogs would prick up their ears in a moment. "No, I can't," my wife might say. "I'm going to places where I can't take them in." The dogs, on hearing this, immediately drop their jaws, and slink under the table, but, whilst the missus has gone upstairs to dress, they both slide off down the park, and lay up under a tree near by the footpath to Stanstead. As my wife passes them they creep up behind her, Help, the retriever pup, and Topsy, the poodle. After a while she catches sight of them, and then Topsy sits up and begs, whilst the pup hangs down his head, and crawls sheepishly towards her; there is no resisting this so she says:—" Come along then." In a moment there is a change from sorrowful pleading to exuberant joy, off they go, barking and yelping like fury, the clumsy pup bringing up the rear, and ending off by rolling down the bank into the stream, where, like a good water dog, he gives himself a thorough washing. Topsy was a French poodle, and very intelligent, as indeed are all his breed, so we never had any trouble with him except once about going with us on a Sunday, and then we did not tell him he wasn't to go.

One Sunday, when I was going to Chapel, I met Topsy down near the street, and he turned back after me. I told him that he must go home for I could not have him, but all he did was to sit up and beg, so I gave him a few flips with my handkerchief, and then put him over the park railings. When I got to Chapel, there was Topsy waiting for me on the step, so I said:—"Well if you'll be a good dog, you can come." I took him up under my coat skirt, marched in, and sat down in my pew, sitting him up on the seat by my side. I held up my finger to him to be quiet, and quiet as a burglar under a bed he was, until the minister said "Amen," and shut up his book, when Topsy kept touching me on the arm with his paw, looking up into my face the while. As soon as the last hymn was given out, I slipped him—Topsy, not the minister—under my coat, and took him out, and that's the only time he ever attempted to come to Chapel.

CHAPTER III.

INASMORE AS TO RETRIEVERS.

TO return, once again, to the Retriever practice.

Bring home a young rabbit, just a runner, turn it down in the room, and let the dog see you turn it loose; as the bunny runs off turn the pup's head away, so that he may not see where the rabbit hides up. When it is "hid up," loose him to find it. You should have the pup in a string, and pull him to you should he stop and play with the rabbit when he finds it; make him bring it you sharply on your calling to him to fetch it.

Keep on this practice for two or three

weeks, then take the rabbit out in the garden and let it run in your cabbage or carrot beds to hide up ; put the pup on the search for it, find it, and bring it to you. Lastly, take the rabbit into a meadow and repeat the process as before.

When the pup is five to six months old, you may try him with a larger rabbit, one that will run for fifty yards before hiding up ; let the pup see it start, and then turn his head away as soon as it has gone a few yards, make him take the scent, seek for it, and bring it to you. You should fire a little powder off as the rabbit is running away.

Next, take a sparrow, thrush, or blackbird, clip his wings, and turn down in the high grass, or in the garden, or in a young wood ; let the dog find that and bring it to you as before.

When your pup gets strong enough to carry a full grown rabbit, get one that is a good runner and stick it in the throat with a pen-knife, like you would a fowl. Let the rabbit go and it will run sixty or seventy yards before it turns up dead ; make the pup search for it and bring it to you as before.

If you live in a meadow or park, you should stick a rabbit as I have described, turn it down at once, fire off your gun, and then run into the house and call the dog, "Here, Help, come on, good dog." Take him out and put him on the scent of the blood, standing quite still yourself, and letting him do the work and bring the rabbit back to you without any assistance. If he is so far trained as to be sure of "finding," take him through the wood and kill a wild rabbit; let him find it out and bring it to you, then put it in your pocket, and go on. As you go along, take the rabbit out of your pocket, and drop it on the ground; walk on for twenty or thirty yards and then send him back for it. After a time go from forty to a hundred yards after dropping the rabbit, then from a hundred to two hundred and so on up to a quarter-of-a-mile, making him go back and fetch it as before.

When you kill a rabbit in a wood, hang it up on a stub within his reach, if you are going home walk from it about two hundred yards and then send him back for it. Increase the distance gradually up to a mile from home, then send the dog back to fetch it when you get home. This can also be practiced by making your dog retrieve pheasants, wood pigeons, and the like, but wood pigeons are the worst kind of birds for the business, as their feathers come out very easily and choke up the puppy's mouth.

One day I remember, my master brought me a new retriever and said :—" Look here, Wilkins, this is a good dog, I bought him off Cotterel, of Takeley Forest, when I was shooting with Mr. John Archer Houblin, but the brute runs after everything; now I will give you £2 to stop her running in after her game." Cotterell had hunted her as a rabbit dog, and she was one of the very best dogs for that work I ever saw, she would catch more rabbits in one day than some bad shots could kill, and she was the best bitch I ever saw, being good all round. Well, I got my £2 for "Duchess" or "Goose," as the Squire afterwards called her, but she got very fat and lazy, and so was sent to Darlington, where, I heard, she was held in high esteem.

I had another dog called "Sailor," who was a rum 'un, but as good as he was rough. I remember the time well, though it is a good many years ago, I was in the meadow adjoining the house, feeding some young birds, when one of the footmen came and called me, saying that the Squire wanted to see me at once. Off we went together and met the Squire on the lawn. "Ah, Wilkins," said he, "I've just come in by train and brought a retriever back with me; he's one of the most savage dogs I ever had anything to do with, I've got him in a crate now, and he won't let anybody come near him, he flies and snaps at their hands with such a vengeance that we could hardly get him out of the guard's van, and we were at last obliged to roll him out on to the platform. At first they got a clothes prop and put it through the crate, but he seized it in his teeth and held it like a vice. I want you to go down and see what you can do, I thought I was about master of dogs, but I can't master this one. Be careful what you do, Wilkins, and mind you don't get hurt."

"All right, sir," says I, "I'll bring him home right enough." So I took my gun and ferret bag, and off I started to the railway station. By the time I had reached there I had made up my mind what to do, so I opened the station door, and there, sure enough, on the platform, was the crate with the dog lying down inside it. Not a soul was anywhere near the crate, so I walked up to it.

"What! Sailor," says I. "Sailor, old dog." To show him I knew who he was, I just raised my gun and flashed a little powder off, cut the crate open and said, "Come along, old Sailor dog." Out he came, I threw him my ferret bag to carry, put his chain in my pocket, and walked him through the streets up to Stanstead House.

The Squire came out to meet me, and saw the dog following me with my ferret bag in his mouth. "Well, well," says he, "However did you manage to let him out of the crate?"

"Oh, quite easily, sir," said I. "I spoke to him as if I had known him for years."

"And he believed you, it appears?"

"Yes, sir, he took it for granted that I was his friend and master." "And you've let him run loose from the Station right up here?" "Yes, sir." "Call him to you now, Wilkins, and take away the bag." "Very well, sir."

So I called out, "Come here, Sailor, good dog." Up he came, and I took the bag from him.

"Now tell him to sit by you whilst you throw the bag away, then tell him to fetch it," said the Squire.

I did so, and the dog retrieved the bag; I took it from him and put it in my pocket, then the Squire and I went for a walk with the dog, and the Squire said, "Now, tell me, Wilkins, exactly how you gained the goodwill of that dog, so as to make him follow you like this." For the animal was as peaceful as possible, and followed at my heels as if he had known me for years.

"Well, sir," said I, "So I will, it entirely depends on the way you introduce yourself to the dog."

"Yes, yes," said the Squire impatiently,

"But how did you introduce yourself; that's what I want you to explain?"

"Well, sir," said I. "I went into the station, and walked up to the dog as if I had known him for years, showing all firmness and confidence, both in him and myself. I called him by name and held out my hand to him, took up my gun, fired a cap and flash of powder, put down my gun, took out my knife, and cut the string of the crate. At the same time, I pushed the corner of my coat into the crate for the dog to smell the scent of game; he at once took me for a good 'game' man, looked smilingly into my face, got up, and wagged his tail. 'Come on, Sailor, dog,' said I, throwing the ferret bag away, and telling him to fetch it, 'Come on, Sailor,' and on he came with me, through the streets up to the house, bringing the bag with him, that's all, sir."

The Squire kept on asking me a lot more questions about the dog, but I said, "I can't tell you any more, sir." "You can answer me this question, Wilkins," says he. "Well, sir," says I, "If I can, I will." "Did he attempt to bite you at all, or show any inclination to do so?" "Not the least, sir." "Now, Wilkins, you have answered that question, but tell me how you account for it, I mean his not showing any ill-temper with you?" "Oh, yes, sir, I can explain that easily enough, I did not give him time enough."

"Well, but how, Wilkins, how?" "You must know, sir," said I, "that I went up to the station door all in a bustle, and shouted to him as if we had been old friends for years and I was looking out for him. Just the same, sir, as if you had gone to meet a train, and as it was starting you saw some friend you had not met for years, and then made yourself known to him; that is how I treated the dog."

"I see, Wilkins," said the Squire, "you made him believe it was a reality."

"Just so, sir," said I, "I made him believe it was a reality, and made him take me for his friend, let it be as it might. And now, sir, will you allow me to ask one question?"

"Go on, Wilkins."

"Well then, sir, if you were a stranger to this

dog and me, and knew nothing about either of us, you could not tell but what he had been in my hands from a puppy, seeing how he obeys me"

"There, Wilkins," said the Squire, "I give you credit for all that." And so we returned home, and put the dog in his kennel.

Sailor was a perfect terror to the Stanstead people, and one of the roughest, most savage dogs I ever met, I always had to muzzle him before thrashing him. To give him his due, he was a first-rate retriever and keeper's dog, properly broken not to run in at partridges, but unpractised with ground game. I should think he had seldom seen a live hare or rabbit before he came to Stanstead, for if he saw one run into the wood, even if it were a hundred yards off, he would bolt after it like a shot. I had to cure him of this, and a tough job it was.

I took him to the peg with an extra strong cord and a check collar on him; the "check" collar, I may mention, is a good stiff leather collar, studded with iron beads, and fitted with buckle and holes. I allowed him eighteen yards of cord, and got my under-keeper to stand near with a sack of live rabbits, while I remained at the peg with my gun and dog.

"Now, George," says I, "Take a rabbit, but don't let the dog see you, stick it, and turn it down in front of him."

Away goes the rabbit, I ups with my gun and fires (half a charge of blank powder), away goes Sailor, hot after the rabbit, but at the end of the eighteen yards he falls heavily. I pull him back to the peg, and make him lay down quietly until I have loaded my gun again, which I do not hurry over doing. When it is loaded, I loosed him from the collar and sent him to look for the rabbit and bring it back to me. This done, I put him to the peg again and repeat the experiment with another stuck rabbit. Bang! bang! and off goes Sailor more furiously than before; this time he is thrown back more heavily, nearly cracking his neck. I tried him once more, and then, as he still bolted after the rabbit, I left off for that day and saved the rest of the rabbits. I tried him again next day, whilst he had the lesson fresh in his mind. You should always follow up this practice every day, until your dog will not attempt to stir after the rabbit, unless you tell him, "Go seek for it," or "Go fetch it," whichever words you accustom him to. If you let a week or more elapse between the trials, the dog will, to a great extent, have forgotten his previous lessons, which is most disheartening, and a waste of time. When your retriever pup is steady at the peg, the next practice is bolting rabbits in the open, but, as this chapter is already outrageously long, I will commence a fresh one for that.

CHAPTER IV.

INASMOST AS TO RETRIEVERS.

CHOOSE your spot where you have your rabbit earths in an open space, meadow, or park, so that both you and your dog can easily distinguish the holes and any rabbits that may bolt from them. Take an iron peg about fifteen inches long and the shape of a marling spike, with a ring in its crown, fitted to travel freely through the hole in the crown, so that when the peg is driven into the ground, the ring will lay flush with the surface. A cord is attached to the ring and fastened to the dog's collar.

The advantage of a commanding view of the

rabbit earths is obvious; hitherto the rabbits have been turned down right by, or close up to the dog, without his seeing them to prevent him chasing rabbits "off a form." Now it is necessary to teach him not to chase rabbits bolted from a hole. Station yourself by the peg, gun in hand, and dog by your side, whilst the under-keeper goes forward with the ferrets to the earths.

The first rabbit appears; bang! off goes the dog, and when he gets to the end of the cord gets thrown as before, and so you keep up the same thing until the dog understands that he must not move until he is told.

After one or two of these practices, I should begin to use the stick to an old dog, and thrash him back to the place he started from, but, if you use the "check" collar, he won't want much of the stick, as the collar will do the trick instead.

These are the simple rules I have invariably followed in training pointers, setters, and retrievers. I have broken many a score of dogs in my time, and have seldom failed to turn them out well-broken dogs. The only dogs I could never do anything with were those whose spirit had been thrashed out of them, or who had been made thoroughly gun-shy; all the patience and skill I possessed was ineffectual with those sort of dogs, and I used either to destroy them or return them to their owners.

Young keepers, when they first take this difficult branch of their duties in hand, would do well to attend carefully to what I have said about the whip. If a man has a hasty and violent temper, however clever he may be, he ought not to attempt to break dogs. With regard to young dogs, most especially I say, "Leave the whip at home."

CHAPTER V.

HOW I GOT MY LAST JOB.

AS I have before related, in 1840 I left Chesham to go into Wiltshire, as keeper to the Rev. Henry Fowle, who took me, without even seeing me on the strength of a recommendation from Mr. Fuller and Mr. Wilmore Ellis. Mr. Ellis was a great friend of Mr. Fuller's, and a nephew of Mr. Fowle's, and he used often to come down to Chilton to shoot with the latter.

In the year 1841, Mr. Fuller-Maitland came down to Chesham to shoot with Mr. Fuller, and as he missed me, he asked my father where I had gone.

"He's gone down into Wiltshire, sir, as keeper to Mr. Fowle," said my father.

"And does he like the place?"

"Well, no, sir, he doesn't," replied my father. "You see his master's a great fox-preserver, and hunts a good deal, and John would prefer to live with a gentleman who preserves pheasants and not foxes."

"Is that so, Luke? I had always marked him for my own keeper; I always thought that if ever I had a keeper, I should like your son John.'

"Well, sir," said my father, "I know John would be delighted to come as keeper for you, he was always glad when he heard you were coming here to shoot.

"Then you may tell him, Luke, that I spoke to you about him, and, if he wants a change I will take him on, but not for two years."

So my father wrote and told me of this conversation, and I at once replied, begging him to do all he could to get me a place with Mr. Maitland. The next year he came to the "Germans" again, and spoke further to father on the subject, when my father told him I was most anxious to get the place as his keeper.

"Tell him," said Mr. Maitland, "that next spring twelve months, all being well, I will take him on." And so I was promised the place two years before I got it. On Lady Day, in the year 1843, I came to Stanstead, Essex, as head-keeper to William Fuller-Maitland, Esq. It was the 25th of March, and I have been there ever since.

CHAPTER VI.

CONCERNING GAME AND THINGS.

I HAVE lately been talking about dogs, and when I once get on that topic I find it difficult to leave off. I wish it to be understood that the rules I have laid down are not of universal application, as different parts of the country require differently trained dogs; for instance, a hilly or mountainous country requires a strong and quick dog, whereas, our country, in the flats, requires a steady and slow dog. A hill-bred dog, again, must have more license allowed him than a flat-country dog; still, the same rules for breaking applies equally to both, and the keeper must be guided by the surrounding country as to whether the dog shall be broken for far or near quartering.

In Wales, Scotland, and the North of England, men may say that the rules I have laid down cannot be applied, as they would make the dog a "close" hunter, where you require a a "wide" one. I say, then, that the dog has to learn his A.B.C. before he can do anything in the way of hunting properly, and the keeper must therefore be guided according to the exigencies of the case, as to how far, and how strictly, he should adhere to my rules.

I am now going to write a little about ground game, and will commence with the keeper's dodges for hares. I do not wish to be thought conceited, but I am only stating the plain truth when I say, that, about these parts I used to be considered a noted man for hares by all who knew me. Mr. Alfred Hicks, one of the tenant farmers, once asked me how it was that sixty hares were all feeding at once in a crab-tree field of nine or ten acres of grass, at half-past three in the afternoon, in the month of November. I never told him the secret, but I don't mind telling it now. You take a pound or more of parsley seed, and sow in the night-time all over the field. Let no one know anything about it, but take the seed in your large pockets, and scatter it broadcast all over the field; the hares will then feed in that field in preference to any other. I have done the same thing on land sown with clover, near the cover, that is, home fields, not those a long way from your woods. This is one dodge to make the hares feed at home, and take to that particular field for feeding. The hares will keep the parsley down, and, even if the farmer does find a sprig of parsley in the clover, he will think that it slipped in amongst the clover seed.

Another great secret in getting hares is to keep down the bucks, who, in the months of March and April, run and hunt the does to death. Kill off the bucks, they do to give away as presents to anyone, as a reward for services rendered in saving pheasant's or partridge's eggs for you. I have frequently seen five or six bucks chasing one doe hare until she dropped dead from exhaustion. I have seen them run a doe hare when she was seeking for a place to lay down her young. You ask, is it possible? I answer that it is, most undoubtedly. I have seen a buck hare not only kill the doe, but literally cut her back to pieces as she lay dead, with, perhaps, two or three young ones inside of her. Thus the buck hares do you an immense amount of harm and injure your stock for next season.

Another great secret is to keep the vermin down. Now I suppose gamekeepers will say, "We know that, Wilkins, tell us something we don't know." To which I reply that there are many of you who know it, but won't take the trouble to do it, and consequently the vermin destroy one-half of your leverets, and they never come to the gun; so you only keep your hares to breed young ones for the vermin to feed on.

"Well," say you. "Anyhow the leverets are useful to feed the young cubs on." True, oh king! I grant you that, and also admit that whilst the vixen is taking a leveret to her cubs she cannot be hunting for a hen-pheasant on her nest. It is true again that we must have foxes, and I know all this without being told as well as you know that it is necessary to keep the vermin down.

Now just allow me to say that, by keeping the vermin "close down," you will have more leverets for the vixen to take to her cubs, and more hares next year for your master's guns and the guns of your master's friends to shoot. Also, the more hares you have the more you will save the hen birds and their nests from the foxes. I had three litters of cubs in Thrupp cover one spring, of nine, seven, and five respectively, besides the old ones.

Mr. Fowle was not only a fox-hunter, but a fox rearer. "Wilkins," he used to say to me, "I will have foxes, if I don't get a single pheasant." "Very well, sir," said I, "So you shall." And during the three years I lived with him, I never shot or trapped a fox, so that when he was giving me a character, he wrote, "He is particularly clever at breeding game and destroying vermin, but is not a fox-killer."

If I had not gone to Stanstead, Mr. Fowle told me that he should have sent me to Salisbury Plain as keeper, to take charge of all his men and keep his accounts, at his place there.

Another thing that keepers often neglect to do is to keep their hares out of the poacher's pockets; and this is either through ignorance or laziness, because they do not sufficiently look after their gates, to see that they are not netted, and their hedges, to see that they are not snared. One simple way of attending to this, is to look more after the hares of an evening and even at night-time, and spend fewer hours at the public-house. I am afraid that this remark of mine about the public-house will not be relished by many, and repudiated by most keepers, but, although it's a dirty bird that fouls its own nest, I am speaking to *all* keepers, and at the risk of giving offence, I shall let the remark stand.

I have heard keepers say that they can learn more in an hour at a public-house, than they can in a week by stopping at home. Now this is a lie that is half the truth. Very likely you may hear that old Pat Lane brought a hare to someone's shop to sell. What then? the hare was dead, and you won't bring it back to life again, or replace it in your cover, so how are you better off for knowing that Pat took the hare to Tom Tills, the fishmonger, to try and sell last week. "Why," say you, "I shall keep a sharp look-out for him." Yes, at the "Red Cow" public-house I suppose, that is the last place in the world to catch a poacher snaring hares, he is much more likely to snare you, my boy, for many a keeper has been snared at public-houses, and the snare drawn so tight as to nearly choke him to death. Not only himself, but his poor wife and children as well have been nearly starved to death by this useless "public-house" dodge of obtaining information. You will get more information by practically attending to your night duties, than you can ever hope to obtain by loafing about in a public-house; there, you will only get a quantity of bogus "tips" and bad drinks, offered on purpose to keep you out of the way, and throw you off the scent.

CHAPTER VII.

MINE HOST AND FRIEND BALDWIN.

IN the year 1843, when I first went to Stanstead from Wiltshire, my neighbour, whom I will call one Jones, had reached there the week previously. I arrived on the 25th March, and he got there on the 18th. He had previously been living near Thetford in Norfolk.

We used to join forces at night-time and help each other at first, as his woods were adjacent to mine at Birchanger village. Jones was keeper to Mr. Fred Nash, of Bishop's Stortford, and a very good keeper he was, and did well for some years, always having plenty of pheasants and so forth. But after a while he began to fall off in his night appointments with me, till at last he never kept them at all. I used to go to the usual place, but he did not turn up, and this happened time after time, till at last he left off asking me to meet him. His pheasants grew gradually less and less, until at length the stock dwindled down to nothing. This was only just as I expected, and so I told him; I remonstrated with him time after time, but when a man becomes dogged in his infatuation, remonstrances are of little avail, until he at length awakens to the enormity of his folly.

Instead of being in his woods looking after the game, Jones was in the public-house at Pine's Hill from ten in the morning until eleven at night. This public-house was called the "Bell," and it lost him his character and place in the end. He had a character, indeed, but it was a bad one; in addition to which he possessed a wife and large family. Drunkenness always stands in the way to prevent obtaining employment, especially as a keeper.

So Jones became a game destroyer, or poacher, and he and I met once more at night. He brought five men with him on that occasion, and I had two with me, so that when we joined forces the gang numbered nine, all told. We had a little bit of sport that night, as I will relate further on. Jones, poor fellow, was one of those keepers who say they can learn more at a public-house in an hour than by stopping at home for a week.

I remember another keeper who used to say the same thing, and whom I will call Baldwin. I admit, friend Baldwin, that you may learn something at a public-house; the landlord is a jolly good fellow, and a very great friend of the keepers; he puts the latter up to the poachers' games a bit; he tells you, now, that Tom Darvell had two hares for sale the other night, in his house—two out and outers they were, regular nine-pounders, and snared, too, he could tell that by the look of their eyes. Five bob the two was what Tom asked for them.

He told you all that, did he? You say he did; very good; but he forgot to tell you he knew it was quite true because he bought them himself for four bob and two pots of beer. He could, if he had chosen, have brought the hares up from the cellar and shown them to you. Did he also tell you that Tom Darvell stopped at his house all day and spent two shillings out of the four? No! Well, anyhow, you are deeply impressed with the news, and turn to go, determined to keep an eye on Tom in the future.

Mine Host takes you aside. "Don't be in a hurry, keeper," says he. "I want to have a little talk to you before you go, I have a lot more to tell you yet; have another glass, old friend, there'll be nothing going on before the publics are closed. You will most likely drop on to some of the rascals as you are going home, but it's no use yet, for they have not left the 'pubs;' eleven or twelve is their time you know, keeper, when they think all is quiet. Look here, can't you manage to get us a day's rabbit shooting next week, just myself and a few respectable friends that will be a credit to you and my house. The Squire's going away for a week or two so I hear, isn't he?"

"Yes," you say, "he goes to-morrow morning."

"Ah, well, run down again in a night or two, and we'll talk it over a bit. Who shall we ask? I don't want a lot of roughs, you know, they'll be no good to either you or me; we want someone that can stand you a tip, and don't mind paying for a good dinner after a good day's sport and cracking a few bottles of good old port; that's the sort of people we want to get you know, keeper, so as to do us both a good turn." So you see what Host Goodman desires to do is to please both the keeper and the shooters.

After a night or two, down you go again and Mr. Goodman draws another couple of shillings out of your pocket; he has pretty well decided by this time as to who this respectable party shall consist of. Young Farmer Hopkins is to come, and a few of the most reckless spendthrifts about the place, not forgetting to make up the number with a couple of the "most owdacious young swells" in the parish, there is to be a real good flare up or "randy-dandy."

It gets noised about that Keeper Baldwin and Landlord Goodman are going to give a grand shooting party, with a noble supper to follow. The poachers have their ears and eyes open, and smell business; they join your noble crew on the night appointed, one or two of them are in attendance at Mr. Goodman's, ready for any little job he or you may want done, and more especially to show themselves to you, friend Baldwin, for don't you see Pat Lane and one or two other well-known poachers in at Goodman's tap, enjoying themselves over a pot of beer. Goodman either lends them a bob, or else trusts them to-night, for he knows that they along with them, will be at his house to-morrow spending last night's booty, so that he will get his money back with good interest; he knows also that these men are at his house on purpose to set the keeper perfectly at his ease. So you see mine host has fleeced you— the keeper—and the shooting party, including the two "swells," not content with that, he must now fleece the very men he's in league with. He's a nice sort of man isn't he? All the proceeds of the night's poaching will find its way into Mr. Goodman's pocket and larder, and the miserable pittance he allows to the poachers, who have risked perhaps their lives, and certainly their liberties, will come back to him eventually.

Now, Baldwin, you say this landlord is a great friend of yours, and makes you "fly" to the poachers' tricks; well, I ask you, what is this man's friendship and information worth to you? Not much, I think. "Why," you say, "we had a jolly evening at the 'Red Cow' after a good day's sport." Quite so; and you lost very much by it. "Lost?" you say, in astonishment, "how, in what way?" Listen, friend Baldwin, and I will explain.

You killed twenty couple of rabbits. Mr. H. took three, Mr. G. took four, Mr. W. took three, and Mr. Goodman took six to make into rabbit pies for the evening party. That makes twenty-six out of the forty, and then, again, you gave Jack Smith one for brushing, and two apiece to two of the young "town swells" who joined in at the supper in the evening. That leaves you nine rabbits for yourself, thirty-one rabbits going to others. Now as to the tips Mr. Goodman talks so glibly about, methinks he has them, and not you. The man who took two rabbits gives you a florin; the one who took four presents you with half-a-crown; another who took two, tips you a shilling, the rest, including the swells, shell out a "bob" each, and the landlord stands brandy and water, and very kindly invites you to come down to-morrow night and have a snack off the fragments of the feast. That is one for you, and two for himself, for he knows that you'll spend half-a-crown or so in the shape of drinks, beyond what he gives you to eat. The rabbits you gave away were worth thirty shillings.

Now, what good have you got from Mr. Goodman's respectable party? How much have you lost pecuniarily? How many hares did you lose, both in the night and in the day-time, when you were with this noble party shooting and feasting? Is that how you learn more in an hour at a public-house, than you can in a week by attending your covers? If so, my boy, I say that you are not much of a keeper—except a public-house keeper, and I should strongly advise you to leave off game-keepering and take the "Red Cow" at once, for you are more fit to be a publican than a gamekeeper. The proper place for a keeper is to attend to his duties and prevent poaching in his covers, and not in the public-house, and this I cannot repeat too often.

CHAPTER VIII.

HARES, RABBITS, AND FARMERS.

I WANT, now to draw your attention to the methods of snaring employed by poachers, and the various ways in which a keeper in the old days, had to meet and defeat the same. I say "old days," because I don't know what effect the recent "Hares and Rabbits Bill" may have, or has had on the ground game, but I do know that wherever it is extensively preserved without an efficient staff of keepers to look after them, there will always be men found to poach them. Poachers have often told me that they mostly take the game for the excitement, rather than on account of pecuniary benefit; it is a very common tale—public-house first, and devilment afterwards.

In Spring, when everything is sprouting afresh, the hares have to cut new runs, especially in the newly-made hedges. When you come across a newly-made hedge, take a good look right along it, and you will find that the hares have made four or five runs through it; if you snare these runs you will probably catch in four out of the five set snares. The poacher-snarer knows this as well as you and I do.

Prevention is better than cure, and as it is obvious that you cannot cure the poacher, you should prevent him, by helping the hares. To do this, you must make twenty good runs through the hedge, resembling the hares' runs as closely as your art can possibly make them. When making these false runs you may carry a hare's leg and a bag full of hare's fluck in your pocket. Cut all small twigs in two, pat the earth down well with your hand, and then make the print of the foot, pricking out the toe nails in the run with the limb you carry.

Hang a little fluck on the twigs of the run, to make believe that Pussy goes through it very often, and serve all your artificial runs in the same way. The poachers will set the best runs, as they think them to be, but of course, being false ones, they will not catch much in them for a time, till the hares begin to find them out and use them. Thus, you see, there will be twenty-five runs in the hedge instead of four or five, it will take twenty-five snares to set this hedge, and so the hares have twenty-five to five, or five to one chances on them. By doing this, you will save many a hare from being caught, and give the poachers a vast amount of extra trouble, and if you carefully "doctor" all the likely hedges in that way, you will be doing good service both to the hares and yourself.

I have before mentioned the "Hares and Rabbits Bill." Before the passing of this Act there was many a bitter word between tenant farmers and keepers, that is on the part of the former, for keepers have to be civil all round. Now I don't mean to state that hares and rabbits do no harm to the farmer, but I do maintain that in many instances, these unfortunate animals have had to bear the blame for things which have been the result of nothing else but bad farming.

I will take the two (hares and rabbits) separately, and show as far as I am competent to judge, the exact proportion of damage they each of them do. Of the two, then, I consider the hare is the worst offender; both are nocturnal ramblers and feeders, but the hare roams far afield, whilst the rabbit never gets a great distance from his burrow. The hare, too, is a destructive feeder; it will often cut down blade after blade of young wheat out of sheer mischief. All fields are alike to her, as she is migratory in her habits, and if she is not "located with regard to cover," she may be here to-day and two or three miles off to-morrow seeking a new home, but once "located" to a cover, she seldom migrates to another one. I have known hares when disturbed off a farm always make for their home cover, even though it be a mile away; but if you continually disturb this home cover by shooting or with dogs, they will soon, if there is any left of them, leave, their place being taken by strangers, after a while.

It will be seen from this that the hare becomes rather a formidable enemy to the farmer, if not kept under proper control by the keeper, as regards feeding, locality, and keeping down the young. As to this, by particular feeding, you will be able to domicile the animal in certain fields, and make certain wooded localities its home cover. I have frequently had a matter of ninety hares in a small copse, not more than an acre-and-a-half in extent, and, what is more, little or no complaint about it from the tenant farmer; but then the cover was favourable to hares, they remaining in it a good deal, and so doing no damage worth speaking of. If hares are not properly looked after by the keeper, the tenant farmer is injured by the destruction of his newly-sown wheat, barley, and other seeds that compose a winter or summer crop.

With regard to rabbits, there is much difference of opinion, and I have not the slightest hesitation in saying that the rabbit is blamed more than he deserves.

The rabbit is essentially a denizen of the wood, save where there is a warren, or earths or burrows in the open, and this happens generally only on park lands, banks, or gravel pits. More especially when it is found increasing rapidly in numbers, the rabbit invariably lives where grass flourishes more abundantly than any other herbage or vegetable matter. A nocturnal rambler, though never far away from home, the rabbit always prefers meadow land to any other, the feeding time being either early in the morning or late at night. He is made very sharp and 'cute by being surrounded with so many enemies from the moment of his birth; ground and flying vermin make him their prey, so it is not to be wondered at that he not only keeps a keen eye on his retreat, but also chooses feeding grounds in such close proximity to his burrows that he can disappear, as if by magic, at the slightest hint of danger. He does not, as a rule, sit out on arable or ploughed land; take a strip of wood, with grass land on one side and ploughed or newly-sown wheat land on the other, and you will find ten rabbits put up on the grass land to one on the ploughed or wheat land.

You will seldom find small woods surrounded by arable land full of rabbits. Why is this so? for, if young rabbits really spoil the wheat, that would seem to be the most likely place for them to settle. On the other hand, take any wood partially surrounded by pasture land, and you will find any quantity of rabbits there. In beating large woods you will invariably see that the rabbits congregate in the beats nearest the meadow lands, rather than in any other part of the wood.

The rabbit is certainly destructive to young trees, more especially larch trees, but nine-tenths of the rabbits that are put upon the table for eating are grass-feeders pure and simple. As there are many different specimens of grasses, he is probably an epicure, but, in a wild state, it appears that he frequently requires a change of food medicinally, and for this reason he may make raids upon gardens, becoming almost a district visitor, if not speedily repressed. For the same reason he may pay visits to the young wheat adjoining his cover; but, in spite of all this, he does not do one half the mischief that the farmers accuse him of. I contend that rabbits can be kept in cover in large quantities, without their becoming a pest or nuisance to the farmers, and especially in large tracts of shooting that are well wooded.

Whether you keep your ground game in the woods or in particular runs, you can always doctor their runs. Mix oil of aniseed, oil of musk, oil of thyme, and oil of spirits of tar, in a bottle; drop a few drops in the runs you don't want the hares or rabbits to use, or paraffin oil will do almost as well.

The farmer can't make out how it is that the rabbits won't come out in his newly-sown barley when he is waiting for them with his gun, but I know why it is, though I don't feel called upon to call him from his dinner to tell him. He complains to your master that the rabbits come out of the wood and eat his barley. I reply that I set snares for them, and he comes and looks at the wood-runs and sees for himself that the snares are set. "They don't catch much," says he. "How is it, Wilkins? The rabbits seem to know the snares are there." "Well, yes, they do." "How's that?" "Most likely they see them standing in the day time." "Ah, I suppose so; I thought they might smell them, Wilkins." "So they do, sir, or they smell where we've been trampling about the runs setting them."

If, by chance, you catch a rabbit in one of these snares, lay a lot of fluck in the run, and make a lot of scrambling about, rub the fluck on the newly-scratched ground in half-a-dozen of the runs, and hang a bit of fluck in the eye of the snare as if it had caught. You do all this, of course, early in the morning. You meet Mr. Rabbit Complainer in the course of the day:

"So I see you had some of them last night

in your snares, Wilkins." "I set them on purpose, sir." "I am glad of it, Wilkins." "Yes, sir, it will help baulk them a bit if we catch a few of them coming out after your corn." "Yes, yes, it all helps, Wilkins; good morning." If you can only satisfy him, that is something; it goes a long way sometimes, and is one of the tricks of our trade.

So much for snaring rabbits. The squire tells the keeper that foxes he will have, the keeper says that rabbits he must have, so the more harmless you can make them both the better for master, keeper, and farmer. The farmer hunts, so that he should not be too selfish and hard upon the keeper, by complaining about the rabbits; he ought to know that everything in the way of game rearing must be taken fairly with fox preserving, and, being a hunter, he has no business to complain of rabbits. On the contrary, he must help keep a few rabbits to feed the foxes on, for while the vixen is taking an old doe rabbit to her cubs she is not hunting for a hen pheasant on the nest or robbing the farmer's hen-roost.

CHAPTER IX.

POACHERS' DOGS, AND HOW TO KILL THEM.

A GREAT dodge in poaching used to be gate netting. A hare on the prowl, started off a field when feeding, generally makes for the gate-run—that is to say, leaves the field by means of the gate—and, for this reason, one of the oldest methods of poaching is gate snaring or netting.

To prevent this you should tar the lowest rail of the gate, so that when the hare goes underneath it she smears her back; she will then avoid the gate for the future, and find some other way in and out of the field, for whichever way a hare comes into a field at night, she will go out the same way if she possibly can. Now the hares, thus driven to avoid the gate, make through the hedges, and the more runs there are through the hedges the more chances there are for the hares, and the less for the poachers. Thus you protect the hares and baffle the poachers. Finally, fasten the gate with a good strong wyth, and put a peg through the framework.

Poachers, when after ground game, are invariably accompanied by a dog, which is generally a mongrel of the hound species. As I think I have before mentioned, it is of the utmost importance to get rid of this dog somehow or other. If you can do this it will often break up the gang of poachers for the season, as it is generally a very clever dog and difficult to replace.

I am now going to tell you how to preserve your hares from the poachers and their dogs. Set an alarm gun in the field where the hares feed, generally a clover field; place it in the centre of the field, and attach three strings to the trigger, leading them away from it in the form of a three-cornered table, so that the dog is bound to run on to one of the three when driving the hares or hunting the field. Bang! goes the gun, and off run the poachers. "He's shot the dog," they cry, and forthwith catch up their nets as quickly as possible, and make off; if there are two nets, they take the nearest and leave the other, and they do not stop to touch the gate netting.

After they have gone about half-a-mile, the dog overtakes them. "The old devil missed him, after all," is their polite comment; "that couldn't have been Wilkins shot at him, it was one of his men; he'd a' been a dead 'un if Wilkins rose his gun to him."

I only use the alarm gun on nights when I am not watching, and then more to baulk the poachers than anything else. When you are watching the gates it would do more harm than good; it is only of use to prevent the poachers killing your hares when you are not there.

Here is another dodge for poachers' dogs.

POACHERS' DOGS, AND HOW TO KILL THEM.

Take a rabbit's liver, heart, and lights, and season them. Put them into a pound canister tin, and carry the tin in your breast pocket. You will require four livers, or four seasoned doses, and you should put some blood with each dose. Lay one dose two or three yards away from each gate, and, while the poacher is engaged in setting his net, the dog will scent the blood on the dose, come up, and eat it. The poacher sets his net, and then, not knowing what his dog has been about, calls to him:—" Here, Bob, go on, good dog." Away goes Bob across the field, but before he has got a hundred yards he begins to feel very queer and staggery. He winds a hare and makes a rush for her, but, as he is drawing up to her flanks, he pitches a somersault head over heels; he tries to rise, but only falls over again, his legs going out as stiff as iron pokers. It's all up with poor Bob, he never returns to his master, but lays there until next morning. You come to pick up your doses, and find one clean gone. (This is Irish, quite Irish, you know.—EDS.) Look about you, and you will see a great prize; put him in a bag, and bury him with all honours. That gang of poachers is broken up for the season, for it is a hundred to one that they cannot get another dog, and, if they do, it won't be another "Bob," but some animal of very little use to them.

Where keepers are bound to risk everything to get rid of certain poaching dogs, and so break up gangs of poachers, this dodge always answers well, but it is a dangerous game to play, and I don't like it as much as the alarm gun, because, with the best intentions of doing your duty and giving every satisfaction to your master, you may bring discredit upon both yourself and him. For instance, suppose a fox comes through the gate and picks up one of your doses; he is found dead in the ditch or fallow field, and you are blamed for it. This makes it very unpleasant for you and your master. Of course, if there is no hunting, and no hounds are kept in that part of the country, it is the best dodge out to stop gate netting; but, still, I like the alarm gun better.

I make my own alarm guns, and can set

POACHERS' DOGS, AND HOW TO KILL THEM. 227

them in the field or woods so as to make the dog commit suicide, but the same drawback applies to this as well as the doses—a fox may get killed as well as a poacher's dog. It is far better to set them merely as alarm guns, and not load them with shot at all, as a man might possibly get entangled in them.

A great thing in preserving hares is to keep your covers quiet, and not shoot and hunt them continually, thus disturbing the hares. Some keepers cannot make out how it is they have so few hares in their woods, although they are well looked after. John Lawrence, of the Brick Kiln, is as good a keeper to 'look out' as you can well have, as anyone who knows him will tell you, and yet he hasn't many hares. This is because he is always pottering about and disturbing his hares, so they shift to some other run, where they can lay quiet, and do lay quiet.

This is a very important point in preserving hares: you may drive the game clean off your estate simply by disturbing them frequently. Say you have a plantation an acre and a half in size, with a hundred hares in it, as I once had in the Quarter-mile Field plantation; now, hunt or otherwise disturb the plantation four days in the week, and on the fifth day you may find one brace of hares in it, but you won't find more. Yet there have been no hares killed; it is simply the result of disturbing the hares from day to day.

In concluding this chapter I may mention that a few mangold wurtzels and sweet carrots, put in the covers, is a good thing to help keep your hares at home.

CHAPTER X.

A BLOODY FRAY.

AS I have before mentioned, my neighbour Jones lost his place and took to poaching. One day I discovered that a net had been set at Honeysuckle Gate, and another one at Ryecroft Gate, so I and my under-keeper, Joslin, together with George Hutley, went to the former place, where I and Joslin stayed, whilst Hutley went into the next field, about fifty yards further on. About eleven o'clock at night I heard some one coming down the field, and saw three men pass close by where Joslin was hiding, so close that he could have put out his hand and touched them. They came on to my gate and stopped close by me, when I recognised Jones's voice, as he said to his mates:—"You know where the other two gates are, so go and set them while I'm doing this one." The other two then went off into the next field, and Jones remained and set his net between me and Joslin.

After a few minutes, I heard some dogs in full cry in the field, and the men laughing heartily at the sport; then I heard two hares cry out, one in each of the other two gates to which Jones's mate had gone. Thereupon I came out of my hiding place and stepped up to Jones, who was wearing a broad-brimmed felt hat, tied down like a gipsy's bonnet, and also a large cow-dealer's smock gown. I laid my hand on his shoulder, and he hung down his head.

"Is it you, Jones?" said I, "I am sorry to see you here; you are the last man that ought to come to trouble me. I know that you are out of a job, and have a large family to keep, but if you had come to me I would have given you something to help you along."

"I know you would, John," he answered.

I did not take hold of his collar, as he stood perfectly still and quiet. Just then up came Joslin, who was a very big man, and looked at Jones. "Halloa, old chap, is that you?" says he. "Yes," said I, "it is, and I'm very sorry to see him. It's Jones, the Birchanger Wood keeper that was. You take charge of him, Joslin, while I go into the next field."

Upon this he took hold of Jones very roughly by the collar, which roused the latter's temper. "Come, come, gently on," said Jones. He had scarcely spoken the words when Joslin raised his staff over his (Jones's) head, saying: "I'll crack your head open for you." "Go on," said Jones, "Two can play at that game." But here I interfered and cautioned Joslin, saying, as I took hold of his arm: "We don't want any cracking of heads, if you please; the man was civil enough with me, Joslin." Jones, however, was thoroughly roused, so he called to me to 'let be, and that two could play at that game, at the same time putting his nobbled stick in fighting position. There upon I took each man by the collar, and pulled them apart, telling Joslin to simply stand by his man, and not touch him.

Then I went over into the next field, but I had not got more than twenty yards when a lurcher dog ranged past me, at about ten or fifteen paces. I let fly and killed him, and, going on a little further, I came across a net with a hare in it, and a man with a lurcher at his heels. I took hold of the man's collar with my left hand, having the gun in my right, and, as the dog passed in front of me, I shot the dog with the gun in one hand only, never leaving go of the man. I put the muzzle right up against the animal's ribs, and, letting fly, bored a hole clean through him. I then dropped my gun and took up my staff, as I expected to get a blow on the head for killing the dog, but I did not get it, my man behaving civilly enough.

In the meantime I heard my mate Hutley calling out: "Come on, keeper; come on, Wilkins," to which I replied: "Have you got your man?" "Yes." Then I hailed again:

"Have you got more than one?" "No, but do come on." "Have you got your man?" "Yes, come on." "Have you got more than one?" "No." "Then stick to your man; I've got one and Joslin's got another, so each one stick to his man."

"Come on, mate," says I to my man, so I went towards Hutley, and he came to meet me with his man. "Halloa," says I, as soon as I saw them, "Jemmy Boys; old friends meet to-night." "Yes, John," said Jim, who was Hutley's catch, "I wish we hadn't met." "Come on, Jemmy," says I, cheerfully, "this way, please." So we all went to Joslin and Jones, and I said: "Do you know this man, George?" "Oh, yes, I know him well enough," he replied; but he lied, for he did not know him.

After we had searched the three men I told Joslin and Hutley to stay with them, whilst I went and looked up the things, bidding Joslin hold the man we did not know, for I thought we all knew Jones and Boys. I put the nets and two hares in my pockets, took the two dead dogs, one in each hand, and a gun under each arm. Hutley had asked me to take his single-barrelled gun with me, and I had left my double-barrelled gun where I shot my last dog. I was going on, thus loaded up, when Joslin calls out. "Come on, Wilkins, come on, here's three or four more yet." I immediately dropped everything except my single-barrelled gun, and ran up, thinking that Joslin meant three or four more dogs.

"Where, where?" I cried. "Over there," said he, pointing to the hedge. I looked up and saw three or four men, who had come down from the top of the field. I went up to the gap where Jones had set his net, to look at them, when one of the gang reached over the bank with his stick, to crack my head, but I stepped back in time to avoid the blow. I had time, however, to recognize one man as Duckey Phillips, of Birchanger.

"Oh! ho! that's you, Duckey, is it?" says I. "I've handled both you and your father before now, and the pair of you won't make the half of a good man. You'll have about one shot with a stone, I suppose, and then bolt;" for I saw that he was looking which way to slope, and beginning to sidle off.

"Don't get over, Wilkins," cried Joslin; "Don't get over, let them come to us." Joslin was in mortal terror.

I had my sword, which I have before mentioned that I bought off old Dick, hanging by my side. I uncocked the single-barrelled gun, and thought I would throw it away and keep my sword, but, on second thoughts, I threw away the sword and kept the gun, for I knew what I could do with the former.

I had practised single-stick in Wiltshire, and that very night, before leaving home, I had shown Hutley and Joslin what I could do with my weapon. I noticed them smile as I buckled it on, so I drew it, and remarked that it was a very handy thing to carry. I placed the candle on the table. "Now," said I, "I'll snuff that candle backwards and forwards, and then split the wick down the middle, with my sword." This I did, and they then ceased to smile.

Well, I stepped back into the field for a run

up the hedge, which was from eight to nine feet high. I called out to Joslin to let go his two men and follow me. This he did, shouting to me, valiantly and lustily, to 'Go on.' I went pelting up the bank, he close at my heels, and caught a blow on my left temple, which knocked me backwards into his arms. He caught me round the waist, and, being a very strong man, held me over his head with great ease, as a shield against the two poachers above, who then used their sticks on my body, right and left.

Duckey bolted, as I thought he would, and, on seeing this, Joslin threw me down on my face; and next morning you could see the prints of my hands, fingers, and teeth on the ground where I had fallen. Away goes Joslin about twelve or fifteen yards behind Duckey, and the latter, thinking he was being chased, and finding his pursuer gaining on him, fell flat on the ground, and so Joslin flew past him.

When Joslin threw me on the ground the two poachers kept me there with their knobbed sticks, thump, thump, like two blacksmiths at the anvil. I frequently endeavoured to rise, and was knocked down again and again, but at last I managed to stagger to my feet, holding my gun, and with this I struck a smart jumping blow at one of the men. He bobbed his head and put up his hand to save himself, and the gun struck him on the thumb-nail, cutting it nearly off. This did not, however, stop the blow, for the gun-barrel struck the ground at our feet, breaking short off at the stock, and causing me to fall forward on my hands and knees. Then it was thump, thump, thump on my head again; more anvil business. I had a tough job to get on my feet again, but I managed to at last, having the butt of the gun left to defend myself with.

Now ensued a sharper fight than before. I warded off a good many blows, not only with the butt end of the gun but also with my left arm, so that after a time the latter got numbed, and I knew that one of the bones was broken, which turned out afterwards to be the case. I used the stump of the gun so quickly from right to left that I warded off five blows out of six, so that they struck the butt and my left arm four or five times to one blow on my head. Hutley told my master afterwards that I received enough blows on my head to kill a horse, but he was mistaken; he said that the blows sounded like a man threshing on a barn floor, but that was when the gun, and not my head, was struck.

Hutley stuck true to his three men, Jones, Boys, and the man whom we did not then know, but who afterwards turned out to be one George Newman. Hutley did all that could be expected of him, and, had Joslin done as well, we might have got through all right without my being left in the ditch for dead. I kept on defending myself as well as I could, until a heavy blow on the head knocked me over the hedge and into the ditch, insensible.

Big Joslin had run away fifty yards, to the gate where the hare was caught, and where I had collared a man with my left hand whilst I shot the dog with my right. He told me afterwards that he stood there, resting his elbow on the gate, with his head to his hand, or his hand to his head, watching me fighting, till he saw me fall over the hedge, into the ditch. Then he bolted, and the two men with whom I had been fighting, seeing him run away, chased him and drove him up into Bury Lodge Road. There they threw their sticks at him, striking him in the back as he was running away, and that was all the blows that Joslin got.

The men then came back to where I lay groaning in the ditch, and I indistinctly heard one of them say: "Here's a chap in the ditch, kill the devil, drag him out and settle him." "Where is he?" said the other, "I don't see him." "I know he's there, for I heard him groan; that's where he is, bring him and settle him." "I don't see him."

Then I held my breath, as they poked their gate net stick into the ditch, and I felt it scrape over my legs and punch into my calves. "I felt him then; bring him out," said one, and the other forthwith got down into the ditch and began to pull me out. I was too badly battered to care much what they did with me now, and I was perfectly resigned to my fate, when suddenly I heard a shout.

"Stop, Tom, stop, I say; hold hard, let him be; leave him alone, I tell you." It was Jones who spoke, and he came tearing across the field with a vengeance, to prevent them from killing me. "I won't have it, Tom," said he authoritatively, "I'll fetch you down if you offer to touch him." I could tell, by the way he spoke, that he had his stick raised and ready for use. Thus he saved my life, or rather he was the instrument in the hands of Providence that effected this; for when I heard the man coming down into the ditch to kill me, I, in my crippled and defenceless state, cried in silence to the Lord to save me from their violence. I knew it was no use appealing to them, so I called upon the Lord, who holds the lives of all men in His hands, and I did not call in vain, for it was just then that Jones called out to them to stop.

"Come," Jones went on, "we must take these dogs away." "Cut my nail off first, be-

JONES STOPPING THE OTHER POACHERS FROM KILLING WILKINS.

fore we go any further," said the man whom I had struck on the hand. So I saw them cut his nail off, and he left his nail behind, and I left my blood in the ditch. Hutley bolted, after Joslin had gone, which was the best thing he could do, as he was one man against six poachers. He met Joslin at Stanstead, and the two went first to Inspector Scott, and then to Dr. Menasseh Brooks, and told them they had met with a gang of nine poachers (lovely liars), that they had been fighting in a most desperate way, and that Wilkins was killed and lying dead in a ditch at Ryecroft.

CHAPTER XI.

THE SEQUEL TO THE FRAY.—JOSLIN'S DONKEY.

AFTER the poachers had taken away the dogs, hares, nets and gun barrels, I rested for fifteen or twenty minutes, and then made an effort to rise and get out of the ditch. I first got upon my hands and knees, and remained there for about five minutes; then I made a move to crawl out, but only fell back again. I had another long rest until, after repeated attempts, I managed to get out, though not without great pain and difficulty. I was, of course, very weak from loss of blood, and giddy from the blows on my head, and my left arm was broken, so I lay on the grass for ten minutes or so. At the end of that time I got up and tried to walk straight along the hedge, but instead I ran off several yards to the right and fell down.

After another rest I got up again, and although my head every now and then went boring in the wrong direction, and I staggered like a drunken man, I managed to get into Church Road, about two hundred yards from Stanstead. Here I met Inspector Scott, Dr. Brooks, Joslin, Hutley, and seven or eight other men, who were coming to fetch my dead body out of Ryecroft ditch. They took me home, and Dr. Menasseh Brooks examined me and plastered my wounds; he then went upstairs and told my wife not to be alarmed, but I had met with some poachers. "Is he hurt?" enquired my wife, anxiously. "No," lied the doctor, "He's down below, smoking a pipe with Inspector Scott, and telling him all about it; he won't be up for half an hour or so."

Hutley and Joslin had told Inspector Scott how desperately they and I fought with the nine men, "Oh! I was fetched down like a dead man, did'nt you see them knock me over the gate?" said one to another. Now, as I have before mentioned, Hutley behaved fairly well, but he did not get a single blow throughout, and Joslin was not struck at all, except when the poachers threw their sticks at him as he was running home to his wife, poor fellow, to take care of him.

The next day Inspector Scott found the dogs I had shot in a neighbouring pond, about two hundred yards from the place where I shot them; they were identified by the Bishop Stortford police and others, as belonging to Tom Newman, George Newman and Tom Curtis. It was proved that Newman, Curtis, Duckey Phillips, and Jemmy Boys were all at the Clay Pond public house in Bishop Stortford that evening, they all leaving about half-past ten.

The landlord's son came forward to give evidence against them, and declared that he heard them say that they would kill any man who tried to take them, or, rather than be taken they would die first. As I have before mentioned, we only knew three of the men at the time, the two Newmans and Curtis being strangers to us, but Duckey Phillips split on all the rest. He told all he knew, and corroborated the evidence of the publican's son, whose story confirmed Phillips' account.

After laying by a fortnight, I was well enough to go down to Saffron Walden and give evidence before the magistrates; all six men were sent for trial to Chelmsford.

At the trial, Jones, being the eldest man of the gang and considered the ringleader, was brought up first, the others following him up to the Bar. He looked round at the witnesses and, when he saw me, he nodded politely, waved his hand, and his lips mouthed " How d'ye do, John ? " I nodded back to him, and the people in Court looked first at him and then at me, astonished to find the prisoner hailing the witness, and the poacher saluting the keeper. They understood it well enough later on, when they heard the evidence as to how he saved my life.

Duckey Phillips turned Queen's Evidence, and so was let off, but the other five men were all found guilty. In sentencing them the judge said:—"Jones, as you showed mercy to the keeper, and stopped the rest from doing violence to him—probably murdering him—thus saving his life, I shall show mercy towards you; the sentence of the Court is that you be imprisoned for six calendar months with hard labour. You, Boys, who took no action either way, to stop the fight or to encourage it, are sentenced to twelve calendar months' imprisonment with hard labour. As for you, Thomas Newman, George Newman, and Thomas Curtis, the sentence of the Court is that you serve five years penal servitude."

Duckey, the most rotten scamp of the lot, got off scot-free, and came to see me two or three days afterwards. Jones came to see me the day after he got out of gaol, and Jemmy Boys paid me a visit two days after his twelve months were up; he brought me a trap of mine that he had stolen one night when out poaching on my land. The two Newmans and Tom Curtis were let out after serving three years, on account of good conduct, and they all came to see me on their release. Duckey and Boys subsequently left the neighbourhood.

The two Newmans never did any more poaching, but became respectable and sober men. As for Curtis, I've been to his house many a time, and smoked a pipe with him as if we had been two brothers. At Jones' request I went to his old master, F. Nash, Esq., of Stortford, and asked Mr. Nash to try and do something for him. He very kindly consented to do so, and got Jones a situation as tunman in the Stortford brewery, which post he held to the day of his death.

Jones always used to come over, or send me a line of warning, when he heard that any party was going to trouble me. He would sometimes come over on a Sunday morning and go to Chapel with me, stopping afterwards to have a bit of dinner and smoke a pipe. If I had any rabbits by me I would give him one or two, and so we always parted good friends.

"Good-bye, Wilkins." "Good-bye, old friend."

I find I have made a mistake about the two Newmans and Curtis; they were sentenced to seven years apiece, and were let out after serving four only.

Joslin was reckoned the strongest man in Stanstead, and, before this poaching job, no one dared give him back an angry word. He stood six feet high, and was broad in proportion; I've seen him take an ass by the mane and tail and lift him about as easily as if it were a little dog.

One day he was going along the road to Stortford, mounted on his own donkey, which was a good-sized animal, when he came to the turnpike gate just past Zion House. He asked the pikeman how much would be charged for his donkey to walk through. "Twopence," was the reply. "And how much do you charge for carrying a parcel through the gate?" "Nothing," says the pikeman. "Whoa, ass, whoa," cries Joslin, and, quietly dismounting, he deliberately slips his head under the animal's belly, and seizing his fore legs with his hands, lifts him off the ground and carries him through the gate, setting him down on the other side. "Gee up, Noddy," says he, getting on the donkey's back, and on he goes.

CHAPTER XII.

HAGGY PLAYER CAUGHT AND LOST.

I WAS out one night with Joslin and old Daniel Mumford the woodman, when we caught two men gate netting at Gravel-Pits field. Joslin showed the white feather then, and would not face the stick that Haggy Player had in his hand, but kept the two men up in the corner of the field until I arrived. I took the stick away from Haggy, and was gathering up the nets, when Joslin began to bestir himself bravely, and collaring Player by the neck shook him like a rat, saying:—
" Come, let's have none of your nonsense,

HAGGY PLAYER CAUGHT AND LOST. 251

Master Hagg." He knew Charley Player, commonly called "Hag," for I had struck a light with my "identifier" previously, but we neither of us knew the other man.

Haggy said he would not go with me; I said he should, dead or alive, and I tried to induce him to go quietly. No, he'd be d——d if he go for me or forty such men as me. "All right," says I. "We'll see all about that, Hag. Joslin just cut two good strong withes for winding." "What d'ye want with them, Wilkins?" asked Joslin. "Why, I mean to wind them round Hag's shins and draw him to my house; one withe on your shoulder and one on mine, and you and I will draw him home on his back." "I'm sure I shan't take all that trouble about him," says Joslin. With that he whips off his scarf, flings it round Hag's neck, gives the scarf two or three twists, and fetches up Haggy on his shoulder like a hare in a snare, and just about as easily.

Hag began to gasp, for he was almost strangled, but Joslin ran off with him over his shoulder across the field for home. "Ow, ow, Jos—lin, I go, I go," yelped Haggy; so Joslin set him down, and he walked the rest of the way to my house like a lamb, the other poacher doing the same.

I and my guests reached our destination, when I told Joslin to go down to Inspector Scott and fetch him up, whilst I put the frying pan on the fire. "You'll be back by the time I've done the meat," said I. Off went Joslin, but soon came back again to say that Inspector Scott was not at home, so we all five sat down to supper and had a good snap, followed by a pipe and a drop of beer.

After we had been there about two hours, I said:—"Inspector Scott will be in by now, Joslin, so you and Mumford stay here with our two mutual friends while I go down and see him." Away I went and found the Inspector, who had just reached home; he started out with me, and, just before we reached my home, we met Joslin.

"Where's Hag?" says he. "Why you ought to know that, seeing I left him in your charge," says I. "Surely you've not been fool enough to lose him." "Oh, no, he's round this tree I expect," says Joslin, looking round one tree and another. "He's here somewhere." "Not he," says I. "He's on his way to Stortford by now." So Scott and I tramped to Stortford, which was about five miles off, and searched all the lodging houses, but could find no trace of Haggy.

He went up to London, got work in the Docks, became a steady man, and married a good respectable woman. After a while he took a public house at Woolwich, and made quite a little fortune. He used often to come down to Stortford with his wife and daughter, like a gentleman, and bring them to take tea at my house.

"Ah!" he would say, "that was the best thing that ever happened to me when you caught me at the Gravel Pits field, Wilkins, and Joslin let the bird slip out of the cage." And then he would go on to relate how he took his hook, and walked straight up to London that same night.

Joslin was very much chaffed about the

affair. One would cry out:—" Who let the bird out of the cage?" as Joslin was passing; then some one else would start whistling a bird tune.

I had no occasion to complain, for it was a very good slip, both as regards Mr. Player and myself, since he was never any more trouble to anybody. Had we kept him he would probably have got six months in Springfield Gaol, the same as his mate did, and after that he would most likely have taken to poaching again.

Before I finish this chapter I must say a word or two about Jones. Before the poaching affray related in the tenth chapter, and when he was out of a place, I used often to meet him in Bishop Stortford, and he always seemed ashamed of himself, and tried to shun me. I would never allow him to do this, but would always nail him and take him into the " One Star " public house, and "stand" him a good dinner, with a pipe and glass afterwards. If I was very " flush " of money I would " tip " him a shilling, and always, when I wished him good-bye, I used to say:—If you send one of your children over on Friday night or Saturday morning, I'll give him a couple of rabbits for your Sunday's dinner." And he would reply:—"Thank you, John, I will send over for them, and thank you very much."

This was what I had in my mind when I first recognised Jones the night of the fray, and said:—" Is it you, Jones; you're the last man that ought to come and trouble me; I know you are out of a place and have a large family, but if you'd come to me I would have given you something." To which he replied—"I know you would, John." No doubt Jones thought of my kindness to him, when he stopped the poachers from killing me, though he might have thought of it a little sooner.

CHAPTER XIII.

JOSLIN AS A WITNESS.—DUCKEY PHILLIPS.

I FORGOT, in my tale of the poachers, to say about the preliminary enquiry before the magistrates, so I will now endeavour to repair the omission.

There were three magistrates sitting: Lord Braybroke; Squire Smith, of Shortgrove; and Captain Byng, of "The Views," Rickling. Joslin especially distinguished himself as a witness. Captain Byng questioned him about his running away, and he answered that Duckey Phillips was running just in front of him, and falling down, so that he had a hard job to keep from treading on him. "Well," said the Captain, "That's just what you did do, I should think, to secure him. Of course you made sure of him, Joslin?"

"No, I didn't touch him, sir," replied the big man, with a pleasing smile of self-satisfaction.

"What did you do then?"

"I run by him."

"So you kept running away from him?"

"Yes, sir." Joslin was quite unabashed.

"You did not stop to secure him?"

"No, sir."

"Why not? Surely you might have secured him, he was all alone, was'nt he?"

"Yes, sir, there was no one nigh but me."

"And he lay flat on his face on the ground, you say?"

"Yes, sir."

"Then why on earth didn't you lay hold of him and secure him, you could not be afraid of his injuring you whilst on the ground in such a position?"

"Well, sir, there were so many of them, I was afraid there were more coming, so, you see, I ran off and left the lot." And Joslin seemed very proud of his sagacity.

"What, your mates and all?"

"Yes, sir," said Joslin with the utmost complacency.

"Good security for yourself, but bad policy for your mates, I must say, Joslin," remarked Captain Byng.

The Captain told my master, Mr. Maitland, afterwards that he never heard any man admit his cowardice so shamefully as Joslin did. All this occurred considerably over thirty years ago, and both Joslin and Jones have been dead for more than twenty years.

I am obliged to mention Duckey Phillips once more, though he's barely worth the trouble, if only to show the ingratitude of the man. He was called "Duckey" because he was a poor, duck-hearted chap; a most rotten sort of man, who would sell his father or mother for sixpence.

About a year before the great poaching affray I have related, I caught him snaring. I was engaged in watching a snare with a rabbit in it, when I saw Master Duckey come and take both rabbit and snare. I showed myself, and took the rabbit away from him. "Now give me the snare," said I. "I havn't got it," says he. "What have you done with it then?" "I threw it away." "Where?" "At the place I took the rabbit. I did not set the snare, but as I was walking along I heard something scrambling about in the ditch; I looked down and saw the rabbit kicking, and, thinking it was caught in the briars, I took hold of it, and found it was a snare. I threw down the snare, for it's no good to me, I don't use snares."

"Well Phillips," said I. "Come back with me and show me the place, and, if I find the snares as you say, I'll let you go." "Will you?" said he, eagerly. "Yes, I will." "Very well, then," said he, beginning to move off, when a thought struck me, and I laid hold of him.

"Stop," said I. "I will first see whether you have got the snare about you." So I searched him, and found the snare, and seven more besides, concealed about his person. "There," said I, holding it up, "That's the snare you took the rabbit out of."

At this juncture up comes my under-keeper, Tom Bitmead, whose last place was at "Park Place," Henley-on-Thames. Bitmead had been watching some more snares round the corner, about fifty yards from me, and had seen Duckey take up six or seven of these before he collared the rabbit, so the latter was fairly caught.

I summoned Phillips, and he had to appear before the Bench at Walden. He dressed up in his best clothes, and asked me, before going into Court, not to say anything about finding the other seven snares on him. He said that if he got over this job he would never do any more snaring, and that, if he heard that any poaching was going to be done on my land, he would let me know of it in time; he could help me a good deal in that way, and would do, if I did not hurt him unnecessarily now.

"Pray, Wilkins," said he. Don't say a word about those other snares, and you shan't be a loser by it I promise you." "Well, Phillips," I replied. "If the magistrates don't ask the question I won't name it, but if they do I must answer; for remember, I am sworn to tell the truth, the whole truth, and nothing but the truth. It would be just as wrong for me to say that I did not find any snares on you, as it would be if I swore that I found two hares on you, when I did not."

"Wilkins and Phillips," a policeman calls out, and we marched into the magistrates' room. I gave my evidence, and said nothing about the seven snares, for I was only asked about searching him for the rabbit and one snare. Phillips told the Bench much the same tale he had told me, about seeing the rabbit kicking in the briars, and how he was tempted to take it, thinking what a nice pie it would make. "And wouldn't you have done the same, gentlemen, in my place; I hope, gentlemen, you won't be hard on me; I have never been before a magistrate before, and, if once I get out of this, you shall never see me here again. This will be a caution to me never to touch a rabbit. I hope you won't send me to prison, gentlemen, for if you do I shall lose my place at Mr. Brown's."

The magistrates here asked him if Mr. Brown would keep him on in his employment if he were not sent to gaol. "Oh yes, gentlemen," said Duckey. "He has promised that, for he knows I'm not a poacher."

"Wilkins, said Captain Byng. "Do you know anything against this man; have you ever caught him before?" No, sir," I replied. "I know nothing about him except this case." And then I overheard the Bench talking it over.

"He seems a very respectable young man, he is dressed neatly and cleanly, and his employer is willing to keep him on. He can't be a very bad sort of man, for Wilkins knows nothing against him before this case."

So after a short consultation, the chairman addressed the prisoner. "Now, Phillips," said he, "We've taken into account the fact that you are in work, and what you say about not setting the snare; also everything else you have said, and we hope it is all true. So we have decided to deal leniently with you, and inflict a fine of two-and-sixpence; and we don't expect to see you here again."

"No, sir," said Duckey, "I'll take good care of that, and thank you kindly, gentlemen." After leaving the Court he went to the "Hoops" Inn, and got a good dinner out of me, walking home with me to Stanstead afterwards. He was profuse in his promises as to how he would repay me for my kindness towards him. He carried out his promises by bringing Jones, Boys, Curtis, and the two Newmans after my game, and leaving me in the ditch for dead.

CHAPTER XIV.

DUCKEY'S FATHER.—HIS DEATH.

TOM BITMEAD found a lot of snares set in Ladymead's hedge one day, so he and I set to work to watch them, he at one end and I at the other, my end of the hedge being very wide and thick.

Presently, up comes old Phillips (Duckey's father) and looked at the snares I was watching; he did not touch them and passed on, and then Tom Bitmead arrived, and said:—" He's taken up my snares, has he touched yours?" "No," said I, "He merely parted the hedge and looked at mine." "Well, he's taken mine away," said Tom; so we went off together, and found Phillips sitting on Ladymead's stile, lacing up his boots.

I asked him for the snares, and he said that he had not seen any. I searched him thoroughly, but could not find anything; I made him pull off the boot that was still unlaced, for I thought that perhaps he had heard us running after him, and had pushed the snares down into his unlaced boot. They were not there, however.

"Are you sure he took them, Tom?" I asked.

"Yes," said he. "I saw him take hold of the snares, and when I went to look, they were all gone." So I had another good search of Phillips, taking off his hat, and hunting in his breast, his breeches, and everywhere, but no snares could I find, and therefore let him go.

I told Tom he must have made a mistake, and, together, we went to the place where the snares had been set. On arriving there I found that they had not been taken up at all, Phillips having merely slipped them down by the side of the stakes they were tied to, and pushed them under the grass, in order to save tying and untying them again when he set them again for the night. Anyone looking carelessly in the run of a daytime, would not have seen the snares.

Old Phillips was summoned, and had to appear before the magistrates at Saffron Walden. Tom Bitmead and I gave our evidence, and when Phillips was asked if he had anything to say for himself, he swore that he had neither seen or touched a snare on the night in question. He held out his arm, and said he hoped it would drop off his body, and that he might be struck dead, and fall into the lowest pit of perdition, if he had ever touched, or ever seen a snare. The magistrates were horrified at his abominable language, and stopped him from saying any more, by sentencing him to a term of imprisonment.

He told his master, Mr. Sparks, of Birchanger, the same tale he told the "Beaks," and Mr. Sparks asked Inspector Scott what sort of men Bitmead and I were, for he half believed Phillips' tale. However, when he came out of gaol, old Phillips owned up to Mr. Sparks that his punishment was just.

Some few years afterwards, his blasphemy before the magistrates was terribly punished, and his awful wishes fulfilled, showing that the warnings of the Almighty cannot be treated with continuous contempt. "He that hardeneth his neck, being often reproved, shall suddenly be destroyed, and that without remedy."

Old Phillips had a curious and terrible dream one night, and it made such an impression on him that he related it to his mates in the harvest field next day, for it was harvest-time. They were at work in the field, and at noon they sat down to dinner, when Phillips related his dream. He said he dreamed that he was minding a team of horses and a waggon in the field, carting the harvest; he described the field and a few of his companions then around him, all of which he saw in a dream. He went on to say that he took hold of one of the horses by the leading rein, was knocked down and killed.

No one paid much attention to his story at the time, but about half-an-hour afterwards, on their getting up from their meal to resume work, Phillips went up to one of the horses attached to a waggon, to put his bridle on, or do something with the bridle. Just at this moment a fly bit the horse, causing him to swing his head round to his shoulder, in order to knock off the fly, when the bridle ring of the bit caught in the hook of the shaft, so as to prevent the horse bringing his head back into place again. This of course very much frightened the animal, which turned restive and plunged about, at length breaking away from Phillips, and galloping wildly off. Phillips was knocked down and the waggon passed over him, crushing his head out quite flat; the wheels carried away his brains and portions of his skull for a long distance, and they had great difficulty in gathering up the remains of his crushed head. It was fearfully mutilated, and they were obliged to collect dirt, stubble, brains and bones, all together, and bury them.

Such was the end of Phillips; he died with

an oath on his lips, "damning" the horse to "stand still" when it became restive, so he was suddenly destroyed without remedy. This happened more than twenty years ago, and I have heard nothing of Duckey Phillips for more than twenty years.

Old Phillips was the only man I ever remember as trying to swear me down before the magistrates. I always made it a rule, before summoning a man for poaching, to have a perfectly clear case against him, always allowing him the benefit of any doubt, before issuing a summons.

CHAPTER XV.

CUBS, FOXES AND VIXENS.

I AM now going to speak about preserving foxes, breeding cubs, feeding young cubs, keeping them at home, and as to treating the vixen, with other matters.

If you live with a gentlemen who is a fox rearer, and will have foxes, do your best to rear them, for one brace of foxes is more to him than twenty brace of pheasants. I speak from experience, as I once lived as keeper with a real fox rearer at Thrupp Wood, on the Littlecote Estate, Chilton, Wilts. You may be very sure if you live with such a man, that he will prove you, and find out if you are true to him in rearing foxes. I say this as a warning to keepers who take places where foxes are considered before pheasants, and I caution them to be straightforward with such masters, because if they are not their masters will soon find them out.

I was told to look at my earths in Thrupps cover, to see if there were any signs of cubs. I did so, and reported to my master that I believed there were cubs in the large earths by the pit.

"Well," said he, "I will go with you and have a look at them, Wilkins." So he did, and, after inspecting the earths, he said:— "Yes, I think there are cubs; look well after them, Wilkins." "Very good, sir," said I.

After a few days he asked me again what I thought about the cubs, whether there were any or not. I said I still thought there were some. "Are you sure, Wilkins?" he said. "Yes, I am pretty sure of it, sir." "How do you know?" "I shot a rabbit, and dropped it near the earths, sir, and it was gone next morning. Besides, I saw some pheasant feathers, quite fresh, brought there last night."

"Oh! that looks well, Wilkins; it looks like cubs being there. I wish you to look to the other earths in the wood and tell me if you think there are any more cubs in them. Be at the house at ten to-morrow morning, and let me know."

Next morning I reported that there were two more litters, thus there were three lots of cubs in Thrupp cover that spring, consisting of five, seven and nine cubs respectively.

"Wilkins," said my master to me one day. "I want you to go to the pit this evening, and get up into a tree, and see how many cubs there really are in the pit. Come round in the morning, about ten, and report the result." So I went to the pit and made pretty sure that there were nine cubs there.

When I went up to the house next morning at ten o'clock, the Reverend was not at home, but he came in about half an hour later. "Well, Wilkins," says he, "can you tell me the number of cubs at the pit?" "Yes, sir, there are nine." He laughed, "nine, Wilkins?" "Yes, sir, I do believe there are nine." "Come this way," says he, so we walked down the lawn, and talked privately.

"I knew you had been to the pit last night, Wilkins," he began. "For I ran a reel of dark cotton round it, and I have been down there this morning, and found it broken, so I knew you had been there by that." And that is what made him half-an-hour late.

In feeding the vixen and cubs at the earths, your aim should always be to prevent, as far as possible, the vixen taking your game. Rats are very good things to feed foxes on; indeed, some people say that a fox prefers this food to any other, but I am not at all certain of that. It may be that the fox finds a rat the easiest animal to catch, for there is little doubt that a rat caught in the open by a fox has not so good a chance of escape as a rabbit.

When feeding cubs it is better to lay the rats about in different places: one here, another there, and a third somewhere else. Should you lay them all in a heap at the earths, the vixen has no work to do, you have done the work for her in a great measure; she ought to be engaged in taking these rats to her young ones, for, whilst she is carrying a rat to her cubs, she is not spending her time searching for hen pheasants on their nests. Supposing she has taken one rat to her cubs, going back a little way she finds another rat, and off she goes with it to her cubs, then she strikes off in a different direction, and finds yet another rat, and back she goes with this one. All this takes up her time, whereas, if you bring your rats up and lay them all in a heap at the earths, you have done all the work for her; she finds plenty there, so off she goes to worry the hen pheasants, with plenty of time on her hands.

It is a good plan to kill an old buck rabbit, and lay it where the vixen is sure to find it, but don't take it right up to the cubs; in this way you will take up her time, in carrying it to her cubs. Again, shoot three or four young rooks, and lay them about, one here and another there, for the vixen to fetch, and carry to her young.

If you have a hedgehog in any of your traps,

skin it, and leave about in the same way, and the vixen will be sure to find and take it. Nothing is easier to skin than a hedgehog, and the cubs like them quite as well as they like hen pheasants. A dead pig, sheep, or lamb, you may take in the same way, and leave about in the neighbourhood of the earths, for the vixen to carry to her cubs; anything to take up her time, and keep her fully occupied in carrying the food you provide, thus, in a great measure, saving your pheasants.

Keepers should adhere strictly to these rules, never feed in a lump at the earths, or else the vixen, seeing the food ready and provided for her, will grow suspicious and prefer hunting, to taking anything at the earths. We must have a little hunting as well as a little shooting, so keepers should do what they can to keep foxes as well as pheasants, and a great deal depends on their feeding the cubs in the proper way.

Some keepers shoot the vixen and feed the cubs themselves, but you lose a great deal by doing this, and it is a practice I always condemn I know it is a hard thing for keepers to stand by, and see a vixen and half a dozen hungry cubs in the midst of their tame pheasants, and some argue that, if they kill the vixen, the cubs can't get much, only what I bring them, and there's no vixen to kill the hen birds or their nests, so don't tell me that, Wilkins.'

I say that you will lose in both ways, you will lose in young tame birds and young foxes, by shooting the vixen. "What," says you, "I would like you to explain that." I will try and do so.

If you have no vixen, the cubs have no mother to lead them away to other covers some miles off from your's, which she will do if you spare her life. The vixen knew where these covers were, but the cubs don't know anything about them, and they never will, unless they get hunted to them, which is not likely to happen, for they will probably be killed by the hounds before they can find out these covers. Thus your cubs keep to the woods where they were bred and you have them always at home in your own woods, right in amongst your young tame birds, night and day. Six or seven young cubs, playing all the time in amongst seven hundred tame pheasants, will soon work shocking havoc, killing them in the day-time for pastime, and at night for amusement.

This, then, is the result of your own folly in killing the vixen, for had you not done so she would have taken a brace of her cubs to East End Woods, another brace to Ugley Park, and two more to Takeley Forest, six cubs out of your way, feeding on your neighbour's game, and only one left at home for you to keep. Is not that better than having all seven cubs in your wood, night and day, in amongst seven hundred birds?

"Ah, yes," says you. "But there are two ways of reckoning, Wilkins; you have said nothing about how many hen birds the vixen would have killed, had she been alive." I reply:—"that's well worth taking into account, I admit. Suppose she brings three or four a week to her cubs." "Oh! more than that, I have known two, or even three, taken out of Durrell's Wood in one night." "In one night?" "Yes in one night." "Well then, the cubs must have been in a poor game country, and not helped in their feeding in the way I have explained, you must allow for that," says I. "You should take the trouble to feed your cubs, bringing them all you can in the way of rats, hedgehogs, young rooks, jays, squirrels, and old buck rabbits. If you have too many rabbits and have to kill some off, kill a doe rabbit, and give it to the cubs. If you can do all this, you can set down your loss in hen birds at about four a week for one month, that is sixteen old birds killed by the vixen."

Suppose these sixteen old birds brought up eight young birds each, that would make a hundred and twenty-eight wild birds. The tame cubs, for if they have no mother they are little better than tame foxes, will not be easily turned off from your hen coops, often killing the hens and fifty young birds in a single night.

"Fifty, did you say, Wilkins?" Yes, sir, and I say that some keepers have had as many as a hundred and fifty killed by the foxes in one night at the coops. The woods will stink with the dead birds, the tame cubs have killed out of mischief, and left lying about.

It stands to reason that, if their mother is killed before they have fairly done sucking, all their food will have to be brought to their bedside, as you may call it, by their old nurse, the keeper. A man for their mother! they may well be tame, when their mother calls them up to feed, by whistling; can they be anything else but tame cubs and foxes? I say that these cubs, deprived of their mother, will kill more tame birds than the vixen would have done if she had been alive.

So that, you see, although you may think you have acted wisely, when your wisdom is put to the test, you will find that you have less birds for your master and his friends to shoot at, when they come through your woods. Now, what good are these wretched tame foxes to you, or to the hounds?

"Come, come, Wilkins," you say, "They are some good, a great deal of good; when the hunt comes and finds the wood full of foxes, I can plead that to my master as an excuse for there being so few pheasants."

Well, that depends a great deal on your employer, if he is a greenhorn it may pass off all right, but how about the tameness of your cubs, how are you going to get over that? Allowing that the M.F.H. doesn't know a fox from a sandy cat—and that is allowing a great deal—he will surely see that the cubs don't know the country five or six fields off from where they were bred, and that they never had a mother to give them a walk out and show them what a lot of nice covers there were in the neighbourhood. Even supposing that the master is so green as not to notice this, there are plenty of sharp men in the field who haven't a bit of green in their eye, and they are safe to see through you. Aye, and tell you what you had for dinner last week, if necessary.

The huntsman, too, will sniff around you very suspiciously, unless he is a great duffer who doesn't know a hare from a bob-tailed fox. He will know a tame fox from a wild one, as well as you know a tame pheasant from a wild one. When you see the birds come running up to meet you, and peck the corn that you let fall, you know full well that they are tame birds. So the huntsman knows, and can easily tell whether the cubs have had a vixen to train then up or not. Every man to his trade.

These tame foxes are no good to the hunt, they will only run round the wood again and again, and get killed, two or three in one day. "So much the better, if they killed them all in one day," you say. Well, I ask you, is it worth taking all the trouble you have with these cubs? I think not. I, for my part would rather kill the vixen before she lay down her young, than take all that trouble after she has done so, for by depriving the cubs of their mother you have to encounter the following drawbacks.

First, you have to feed the cubs yourself. Secondly, the moment the cub begins to leave the earths, he hunts round home on his own account, in amongst your tame birds, thus causing tremendous loss. Thirdly, these cubs are no good to the hunt because, never having been taught the country, they know no other place but their own earths, and thus, when hunted, they are easily chopped in cover, or else run to earth a few fields from the spot where they took to the open. So they have given you the maximum amount of trouble, and the hunt the minimum amount of sport. Small thanks you will get from the field, keeper.

My advice therefore is—don't shoot the vixen, but help her all you can in the way of food, as I have explained, then when the cubs are 'fit,' brush her about, give her warning that she has been your tenant long enough, and advise her and her family to move off elsewhere. Flash a little sulphur down the earth and she will soon shift, she will take the hint, and move cub after cub away, and when they are all cleared off you will have the satisfaction of knowing that both she and her cubs will do you credit wherever they are found. The other plan, killing the vixen, brings nothing but discredit upon you, but by following my advice you will make many friends and few enemies, and the more friends you have the less you need them.

CHAPTER XVI.

SNARING AND TRAPPING FOXES.

I NOW purpose telling the different methods of snaring and trapping foxes, but it is only for the benefit of Scotch and Welsh keepers, and of such other keepers as live in places where hounds are not kept. I should advise all keepers, where hounds are kept, not to trap or shoot foxes; if any keeper takes to these practices he will soon be suspected and found out, making many enemies and few friends.

"Ah!" you say. "I don't care, my master doesn't hunt." That may be, but the hunting field will make you care. Supposing your master dies, or gives up preserving game, and you are told to look out for a fresh place. You apply to some gentleman, and he casually mentions it to another. "Oh, Wilkins, late keeper at Stanstead, has applied to me to come as my keeper." Now, the person to whom this remark is made happens to be a hunting man, he knows you and your little games with foxes, so he puts a spoke in your wheel, or rather, takes one out. He has an old grudge against you because you are a fox killer, so do you think he will speak a word in your favor? No, no, he will use all his influence the other way, and you won't get that place, simply because you are a fox killer, and for no other reason whatever.

When you were warned about killing foxes you said you did not care, as your master was not a hunting man, but in the very next place you apply for the master does hunt, and, if not, he is certain to have fifty friends who do, and who know you of old. All these fifty will do everything they can to prevent your getting the place.

Still, you say, you don't care. Still, I say, they will make you care, as sure as you are a fox killer. Each one of these fifty possesses fifty other friends of his own, and so your name soon gets bandied about the country, with the nastiest odour attached to it, and that worst of all names for a keeper in a hunting country—a fox killer. Therefore, I say, do not kill foxes, do the best you can without that, and let this be your motto:—"The more friends, the less need of them."

You may say that it's all very well to talk like that, but your master dislikes the name of a fox, and tells you that if you cannot manage to keep your birds out of the foxes' stomachs, you are no good to him. When the hounds come and draw the covers, and find every time they come, he growls at you about being swarmed with them, and so you get wrong that way.

Very well, I know that there are squires and masters who are non-hunting men, and do growl, especially when they see a brace of foxes on foot, when the hounds are in the home covers. There are two sides to every question; in this case plead with the squire, and reason the matter with him, and you can account for the hounds finding in your woods by saying :—"Well, sir, in the hunting season the hounds draw other gentlemen's woods, and thus disturb the foxes, who then shift to other covers. I can't prevent a fox coming from the forest to my covers, and besides, sir, you like the hounds to find in your covers sometimes." However much your master dislikes foxes, he can't gainsay these arguments.

"Yes," he answers. "But I don't want them to find two or three at a time. I like them to find occasionally, and run him, and kill him, then when they come again and draw blank, you can plead that they killed last time, and they can't have their cake and eat it too. Just tell them that, keeper, if they growl next time."

For the benefit of Scotch and Welsh keepers, where no hounds are kept, and foxes are bound to be destroyed, I relate the following methods of trapping and snaring.

Set four spring traps at right angles to each other, so that the bends of the springs touch each other, leaving the faces of the traps set in the same position as the four cardinal points of a compass, North, South, East and West. For the bait, take, a pound of pig's fry liver, and fat the caul and meat; cut it up in small pieces the size of hazel nuts, and fry it in a clean pan. You should do this frying somewhere close to the traps, so as to have the fat hot to throw on the earth, all over the traps, and between them. You may add a little beef dripping when frying the meat. If the traps are set in the middle of a fallow field, walk down the furrow from the traps, and sprinkle the hot fat in the furrow; for this purpose you should tie up a little bundle of twigs, and dip them into the fat, using them as sprinklers. Begin at the hedge where the furrow starts, and go right down, past the traps, to the other side of the field. If a fox crosses the field, he will use the furrow, and, catching the scent, will follow it up to your traps. You might drop a bit of fried meat in the furrow, about twenty yards from the traps, and another piece a little closer, just to let him have a taste before he comes to them.

If you wish to set the traps in a wood, you should follow the same plan, only sprinkle the fat down the ride, each way from your traps. Choose the site where you intend to plant your traps, and then dig a round hole, about three feet in diameter, in two or three different parts of the wood or plantation, or in the gorse field. Take an ash sieve and sift the earth, to take away all the small stones, so that you may have nothing but fine earth to set your traps in. Over each hole scatter some dried old rotten leaves, the larch leaf for preference, and some very fine or dead grass; do not set any traps, but throw your fry on the top of the grass and leaves. Feed him two or three times like this, 'till you see for certain that he goes to the hole and eats the meat, then set your traps, and you are bound to catch him.

You should attach all four traps to a ring, so that they can be pegged down with one strong peg. If you cannot get pig's fry for bait, you might use a pound of real good old Cheshire cheese; cut it up like the pig's fry, only into smaller pieces, and use it in the same way.

Another plan is to take a dead cat, and put it into a hot dung hole, and let it remain three to four days, according to the heat of the dung; take an old pail and put the cat into it, cart her off to the traps and lay her in the middle of them, just slightly covering her over with earth; this will draw any dog or fox to the traps. I have seen a dog, going along the road, catch scent of this bait half a mile away in full wind, and, leaving the cart and his master, go straight off to the traps and get caught.

The cat ought to lay on the manure heap until you can spread the muck out over her, with a spade. Put the dead cat, thus seasoned, into an old hollow stub in the wood, or a tree under which rabbits burrow, push it into one of the holes to the extent of fifteen or eighteen inches, and set one trap at the hole. Do the same thing at an old rabbit earth in a pit, if you can find one, or in an earth in the flat of the wood, an old dead earth that the rabbits do not use, or in an earth on the bank, or in any hole that is not used, and set a trap at the mouth of the hole, six or eight inches from it.

A pig is a very good bait, in a hole, or laid on the fallow field; you might use small pigs, from three to six weeks old, that have been overlaid by their mother. Always balm over your bait with manure before putting it into the holes, fallow field, or hollow stub, as the scent is necessary to attract the fox. A hedgehog will do for bait if you cannot get anything else, but cats, pigs, or dead lambs are the best bait.

In snaring, you have to observe the runs they take, for foxes have their favorite runs in woods, and these runs can easily be found out. To set these runs make six good strong snares, each three feet long, and twist them four times double. Set them in the runs, high enough for hares to go under without touching, otherwise you will catch your hares. Use fine copper wire, which is not so stiff as brass wire, but acts better. If the fox breaks the snare, which he is almost sure to do five times out of six, he goes off with the broken snare round his neck, and in his struggles he draws it tight, and pulls up the eye of the snare, so that it will not slip back to loosen it from off his neck. There the snare will remain, and he has to wear it as a collar until it cankers and kills him, which it will speedily do. Now copper wire cankers more readily than brass wire, and that is why I prefer it.

It is very improbable that you will find the fox in the snare, either dead or alive; I have found one in the snare, dead, but very seldom. It does not matter much whether you find a fox in the snare or not, for, if the latter is broken, you may be sure that he has had his death blow, and is wearing a fatal collar that will soon kill him. If your master pays you ten shillings for every fox's head you get, as some gentlemen do on the Scotch moors and elsewhere, why, of course you had better shoot or trap Master Reynard, for snaring will not assist you much in that case.

END OF BOOK II.

BOOK III.

CHAPTER I.

SHOOTING EXTRAORDINARY.

I PROPOSE, now, to relate some instances of remarkable shooting, after which I shall hark back a little, and give some account of my doings before I went to Stanstead.

I was walking through the village of Elsenham one day, with my gun on my shoulder, when I passed the "Robin Hood" public house, and there I saw Albert Warner, a farmer's son, who lived at Broxted. He was on the spree with a friend of his, taking a glass outside the house, and he insisted on making a bet with me that he would shoot a penny piece thrown up in the air. I did not want to bet, for I knew he would lose, as he was no shot, but he persisted, saying that he was on the spree and did not care a snap so long as he had a shot or two. So I bet him that he would not hit the penny piece; he shot and missed, and shot again and missed, and yet a third time and missed.

"You are only throwing your money away, Warner," said I. "You wouldn't hit one in a hundred."

"I don't suppose I should," replied he, ruefully. "Could you hit one thrown up in the air?"

"Why, yes. I offered to bet John Kendall, the manager of the railway works at the time the railway from Bishop Stortford to Peterborough was being made, that I would hit ninety-nine out of a hundred of anything thrown up in the air. I was to stake my fat hog, which weighed nearly seventy stone, against ten pounds, and I said that Kendall might have nine men with a pound each, or nineteen men with half-a-sovereign each, to join in and make up the ten pounds, if he liked. I did not care if there were forty in the swim against me and my fat hog, but no one along the line dared take up my challenge."

"How was that, Wilkins?" asked Warner.

"Well, they had seen me sparrow shooting with a party of four, when I beat all the four, on Castle Hills. I offered to bet any man a sovereign that I would shoot a cricket ball thrown by him. I was to stand near him, and he might throw it in any way he liked—up in the air, down on the ground, ducks and drakes style, bounding as it went along, back behind him, straight before him, in any way he liked, without telling me beforehand. No one accepted my offer. Then I wanted him to bet me ten pounds that I couldn't hit ninety-nine out of a hundred potatoes thrown up in the air."

"You couldn't hit ninety-nine out of a hundred now, Wilkins," said Warner.

"I know I can."

"I'll bet you a sovereign you can't," said Warner, and I took the bet. We fixed on a day to settle ths bet at the "Three Horse Shoes" public house, Murrell Green. When the day arrived I took my two double barrelled guns and my under-keeper, Humphries, who lived with me at Littlecut, Chilton. I was also accompanied by Samuel Sanders, a baker and grocer, and Henry Pryor, our brickmaker, both of whom have since died.

Well, we arrived at the appointed place and I commenced, using my guns alternately, whilst Humphries stood by and loaded for me. At the fiftieth shot I missed. "Oh, Humphries!" I cried, "there was no shot in that barrel for I did not hit the potato." And Humphries replied:—"Yes there was; I know I put two charges in the gun, didn't I, Pryor?" Pryor assented. "Then you've put two charges in one barrel, and none in the other," said I.

Everybody present crowded around me whilst I 'drew' the other barrel, and sure enough, there were two charges in it. Thereupon a hubbub arose; everybody, except Warner, said that the shot ought not to count for anything, but he contended that it did count, because we had agreed that if I fired or shot at a potato it would reckon, but I was not bound to shoot at any potato thrown up, I might, instead, let it alone and have it thrown up again.

"Never mind," said I, anxious to avoid any ill feeling. "I can win my bet, *now*, but be careful and load right in future, Humphries." So I went on shooting, but at the seventieth shot I missed again, entirely through my own foolhardiness. I had blown many of the potatoes all to bits in the air, so that the fragments could not be collected together, and this made me too self confident and careless. When the seventieth potato was thrown up it fell three or four yards behind me, being badly thrown and everybody cried out:—"Don't shoot, Wilkins." It was impossible to bend my back enough to shoot such a distance behind me, and I ought to have left it, and had it thrown up again. I did shoot, however, missed it, and so lost my bet.

Although I had now lost my wager, the

company urged me to shoot at the remaining thirty potatoes, to see how many I could hit out of the hundred. So, just to show what I could do, I shot two at a time, taking them in my left hand, and throwing them up in the air myself. I hit them all, fifteen double shots, so that altogether I hit ninety-eight potatoes out of a hundred, and as one barrel had no charge in it, I might possibly have hit ninety-nine out of a hundred."

The landlord, Stains, and Sanders, and Pryor offered to back me to shoot the ninety-nine out of a hundred, for five pounds, and Sanders produced a five pound note, but Warner said:—"No, sir, I wouldn't lay against him if you offered to back him to hit every potato out of a level hundred."

Just before we dispersed an Exciseman came up, and took down our names in his pocket book. An account of my shooting somehow found its way into an American paper, and Mr. Henry Wilson, of Stowlangtoft Hall, near Bury St. Edmunds, who happened to be in America at the time, saw the paper, and wrote home to my master, Mr. Fuller-Maitland, about it. Mr. Maitland was displeased, and told me not to do anything of the sort again, and I promised that I would not.

Mr. Bowtel, of the "Rose and Crown," Elsenham, wanted me to go into Bedfordshire to shoot a similar match. He offered to back me for fifty pounds, and give me twenty out of the fifty if I won, whilst he agreed that, in case I lost, he would pay all expenses and it should cost me nothing. I declined, however, because my master would have been displeased, and because I had promised not to do anything of the sort again.

I once took my gun and ferret and went to Durrels Wood, leaving home at eleven o'clock, and returning, at two, to dinner. Between these times I had twenty-one shots, twenty at rabbits, and one at a weasel, and I killed every time, bringing back twenty rabbits and a weasel.

My son Tom, who now lives at Llandrindod Wells, Radnorshire, went out one day with my underkeeper, Alfred Gayler, who is now keeper to Lord Brooke, at Easton Lodge, near Dunmow. Tom had thirty-three shots at rabbits and killed every time, never missing a shot all day, and bringing home thirty-three rabbits. That's more than I ever did.

I have sometimes had fifteen or sixteen shots and killed fifteen. There were three keepers on the neighbouring estates in Wiltshire, Shires, Hobbs, and Maskelyne, who used to say that Wilkins' gun had taken an oath never to miss a snipe. I used to help them kill snipe, when I was at Chilton, as their beats adjoined mine.

Shires was head keeper for General Popham, at Littlecote; Hobbs was keeper for the Dowager Lady Cooper, at Chilton Lodge; Maskelyne was fisherman keeper for Mr. Smith, at the Manor House, Ramsbury. Being a dead nail on snipe, I was always asked to meet them in the water mead which ran all along by my ground at Chilton, near Chilton House and Chilton Lodge. Chilton House is where the Rev. Henry Fowle lived before he went to Chute Lodge, near Andover

Hants, and I was keeper to him at Thrupp Cover. Mr. Fowle rented both house and shooting of General Popham. Major Symons took the house after Mr. Fowle left, and I lived with him for a few months as keeper, but he then told me that he found the place too much for him, and I had better look out for another situation, as he did not intend to remain there long.

CHAPTER II.

THE MAJOR, THE PARSON, AND HUMPHRIES.

I MUST now hark back a little, for I can't always put the horse in the right place; sometimes the cart will get before the horse in spite of all my care, but when I come to jot down over sixty years' experiences some little allowance must be made if I sometimes have to go back on the trail to pick up the dropped threads of my life's story.

I am now about to relate some queer stories of my underkeeper, Humphries, and I should first mention that he left this country, many years ago, and went to Australia, so that

I do not know now whether he is alive or dead.

Major Symons was an Irish gentleman, and all he wanted was cash; he was not overdone with that, I think, for he turned off Humphries, who, in addition to being my underkeeper, was groom, footman, coachman, valet, and anything else in the house and out of it. I liked the Major very much, he wasn't a bad sort of man, but all he wanted was cash. After I had been with him some little while he asked me to bring my book in, which I was very pleased to do, for I had not seen the colour of his money as yet. Before he came to Chilton House he had written to me, to say that there would be a barge containing his things at Hungerford, and directing me to get them carted up to the house, and employ a carpenter to put up the beds and so forth. This I had done and paid for, and I had also found food for the dogs, and paid Humphries six or seven weeks' pay. Everyone in the village was complaining that they had not seen the colour of the Major's money, but when I took in my book on the Friday, according to his request, he settled up all right, paying me every penny, like a gentleman.

I had nothing to complain of in any way, all the time I lived with him, which was only five or six months. He told me, when he paid me, that he would not be able to pay me any more money, but that I might remain keeper for him as long as he stayed at Chilton House, if I could kill enough rabbits to keep myself in lieu of pay. He also told me to go over and see Mr. Fowle, and ask him what should be done with the birds in the pens, as the Major would not want them. Mr. Fowle had left milk white pheasants, pied birds—*i.e.*, red and white—and common pheasants, in the pens, on the understanding that I was to breed up the birds, and then divide them equally between him and the Major. Mr. Fowle urged me to do my very best, and promised me a shilling apiece for the birds he took away. The birds were not to go to Chute Lodge, but to his place at Salisbury Plain, where Parker was keeper, and Mr. Fowle promised me that, when the birds went there, I should go too, to look after them and keep his accounts.

I went over to Chute Lodge and delivered the Major's message, and Mr. Fowle then told me to take a horse and cart, and bring everything that belonged to him and me away from Chilton House; anything not worth bringing away I was to throw down in the street, for some old woman to burn.

"Mind what you are about, Wilkins," said he. "You know what belongs to me, and if there is an old broken hog-trough, and Major Symons has had a new head put on it, knock off the head and leave it there, bringing my part away. Do the same with an old hurdle or box. You can ask Humphries to help you catch the birds, load up the hen-coops, sitting-boxes, and corn." Mr. Fowle had left some corn to feed the pheasants.

I carried out his instructions, and, when I had loaded it all up, I went to the Major, and asked him to be kind enough to come and see that I had taken nothing that did not belong to Mr. Fowle. "You know what belongs to him better than I do," said he, and politely shut the door in my face.

So Humphries and I started off, and he suggested that I should call at the Post Office, and tell them to send my letters on to Chute Lodge. I did so, and Mrs. Smith, the postmistress, gave me a letter which had just arrived for me. Seeing that it was from Chesham I opened it, and read it at once. It was from my father and ran as follows:—"Dear John,—Mr. Fuller has had a letter from his cousin, Squire Maitland, and you are to leave, and come at once. I will meet you at Maidenhead station, next Saturday."

I took my box down out of the cart, and left it at Humphries' mother's house, at the door of which I piled up the broken hurdles and other useless things I had taken away from Chilton House. Humphries walked with me when I started again for Chute Lodge, and he asked me to try and get him the job of killing rabbits for Mr. Fowle, instead of me. He kept on and on, talking and walking, until

I said:—"You may as well go all the way with me Humphries, then you can see Mr. Fowle yourself; I shall come back again to-morrow, so, if he refuses you, you can return with me."

Humphries assented, and we both went on to Chute Lodge, where we were met by the coachman, who told me that Mr. Fowle desired that I should go to him directly I arrived, and that he was then on the lawn in front. Here I found him with his two sisters, and Mrs. Fowle.

"Well, Wilkins," said he. "So you have got here. Have you brought the horse and cart back safely?"

"Yes, sir."

"And have you taken away everything that belongs to you and me?"

"No, sir," said I. "I had a letter from my father to say he had got me a keeper's place, so I took my box and gun to Chilton, and left them there."

"Where are you going to live, Wilkins? What sort of country is it?"

"I don't know that, sir; I only know the gentleman's name."

"And what name is it?"

"Mr. Fuller-Maitland, sir."

"A good name, Wilkins, and, what is more, it belongs to a good family, a very good family."

I think I have before mentioned that when Mr. Fowle told me to bring the pheasants, and his and my belongings, to him, he had promised to find me employment until I got a place. He said that he wanted me to come and kill off his rabbits, as he wished to get up a furze or gorse field as a cover for his foxes; he had sown a couple of fields, but the rabbits had eaten it all up, so he meant to kill the rabbits down until the gorse had time to get up. I might either keep all the rabbits to pay myself, or he would pay the wages he had paid me before, allowing me sixpence a couple for the runners, and a penny a head for those that could not see, beyond my wage. These latter are called 'dead' rabbits because they cannot see, and have to be dug out of their holes; they are worthless except for the ferrets. I might have a man to help me kill the rabbits, but he strongly insisted that I was not to trap them, and, if I snared them, I was to tie a knot in every snare; this was for the benefit of the foxes, so that if a fox got his foot in a snare he could draw it out again. I might snare, net, ferret, or shoot the rabbits, but I was not to trap them.

To resume; Mr. Fowle came down to the stables with me, to inspect the contents of the horse and cart, and there he saw Humphries and asked him what he wanted.

"He has come over, sir, to ask you to let him kill the rabbits, as I cannot do so," said I.

"He won't get that job, I can assure him," said Mr. Fowle, in his pleasant way.

"Well, sir," said I, "I thought there would be no harm in his walking over with me, and then, if you objected to him or wouldn't give him the refusal, he could but walk back with me to-night,"

"You are not going back to-night, Wilkins, I can tell you," said Mr. Fowle. "I want you to shoot, to-morrow; besides, I have got you a lodging, so you can take yourself off into the house and get what you like to eat and drink, and I will see you afterwards. And do you go too, Humphries."

Next morning I arrived at the house at ten o'clock, according to orders, and there I met Watts, the head keeper, who had been with Mr. Fowle and his father for more than thirty years. There were also a lot of gentlemen and brushers, and off we started. When we arrived at the covers, Watts and the brushers turned in, and I was turning in after them, but Mr. Fowle called me.

"Oh, you come here, Wilkins," said he. "Keep by my side and don't leave me all day, except to pick up a rabbit or two I may shoot; I want to have a long talk with you." Then he asked me a great many questions about the Major, and lastly he began to talk about Humphries. "Do you think I can trust that fellow to kill the rabbits, Wilkins? Will he not kill my foxes as well?" he said.

"I never knew him injure a fox, sir," said I.

"I don't see what advantage it would be to him to kill one."

"Why, you know, Wilkins, a fox is likely to take five or six rabbits out of his snares, in one night, so he would lose by that, as I should pay him so much a head for those he killed. Therefore, he might kill foxes as well as rabbits."

"Well, sir," said I, "If you will let him have the job, I will caution him about it." So it was arranged that I should speak to Humphries during lunch time, and tell Mr. Fowle afterwards what I thought about it. The upshot of it all was that Humphries remained to kill down the rabbits.

Mr. Fowle left the gentlemen soon after lunch, and went into the house with me to write me out a character, as I had to leave early, being obliged to walk home to Chilton, a distance of fourteen miles, that night. And thus it was that Humphries obtained the job of killing off the rabbits.

CHAPTER III.

ENCORE HUMPHRIES.

THIS Humphries was a slippery card; as long as he had a tight hand over him he was as good a keeper as most man, but, if not well under restraint, he seemed quite unable to keep straight, and soon got up to his tricks. He wrote and told me that he had dropped into a good thing, earning about two pounds a week for some time; then it came down to one pound, then to ten shillings, and lastly to eight shillings per week. He thought when it came to this that his job was over, and began to cast about for a fresh one, pitching down upon poor Watts, and trying to oust him from his place. This, however, was a bad move, as I shall show.

He dug a pit for poor old keeper Watts—metaphorically, I mean, not literally—and fell into it himself, which served him right. The Bible tells the fate of him who diggeth a pit for another, and such was the fate that befel Humphries, for he fell into his own pit and there remained, as far as keepering was concerned. And this is how it happened.

One morning old Watts came across Humphries as the latter was ferreting, and complained that the foxes took his hen pheasants from the nests; he said that, only the night before, three birds were taken by foxes.

"That's your fault," said Humphries.

"What do you mean? I can't help it."

"Yes, you can," persisted Humphries.

"How so?" asked Watts.

"*Why, put them under the turf.* I put many a one under when I lived with Wilkins, at Thrupp."

"You did?" said Watts, astonished.

"Yes, I did."

"Did Wilkins know of it?"

"No, I'm too old a bird to let anyone else know. Look here, Watts, there's three or four foxes in there, if you like to stand at this end of the cover I will go to the other end and walk down the cover towards you, a brace or so is sure to come up to you, and, if you bowl them over, I'll help you put them under the turf."

Watts was too old a bird to be caught by that kind of chaff. "No, Humphries," he replied. "It would be more than my place is worth."

"Oh, very well," said Humphries. "If you're afraid I'm not, so give me the gun, and you go and drive the wood towards me. I don't mind knocking them over if you do." But Watts was not to be had on that tack, either.

Humphries related this to me himself, afterwards, when he was starting for Australia. "Of course," he said. "If a fox had been killed, I should have split about it, letting

Mr. Fowle know on the quiet. Mr. Fowle would have thought me a good, honest fellow, Watts would go out, and I should take his place."

Humphries made a great mistake when he thought he could take in Mr. Fowle. Finding that Watts would not rise to his first bait he set his brains to work out another plan.

He picked out a spring, one of the best little woods thereabouts for pheasants, and set a line of snares in it from one side to the other; then he went up to the Lodge, and sent in word that he wanted to see the Reverend, very particularly. The butler took in his message, and, after a while, Mr. Fowle came out.

"Well, Humphries," says he. "And what do you want to see me about so very particularly?"

"Please, sir, I've found a line of pheasant snares set right across Murrel's Spring."

"Well, I suppose you have been and told Watts."

"No, sir, I came straight to you."

"Oh! I see, Humphries, you think *I* am going to watch them, and not my keeper, Watts. Go into the house and have what you like to eat and drink, and then take away enough food and drink to last you two or three days into the spring. Watch those snares, never leaving them night or day, and if you catch the poacher that comes to them I will give you a sovereign." Then Humphries touched his hat and departed; Mr. Fowle had set him a hard job, too hard for him to carry out.

Mr. Fowle was a shrewd, far-sighted man, who could see as far as most people through a nine inch wall, and directly Humphries told him that he had not been to Watts, Mr. Fowle saw right through him. Mr. Fowle was then just going away for a few days, and when he returned he sent for Humphries, to ask him how he had been getting on with the pheasant snares. "Did anyone come to them?" he asked.

"No, sir."

"What! No one?"

"No, sir."

"How long did you watch them?"

"Three days and two nights, sir."

"Did you leave them at all during that time?"

"No, sir."

"And you never saw anyone in that wood all the time you were there? How about Watts, didn't he come through, during the three days?"

"No, sir."

"Oh! very good," said Mr. Fowle, and, with that, he sent Humphries away, and went to Watts, telling him what Humphries had said. "And you, Watts," he concluded, "have never been through that wood all the time."

Poor Watts stood aghast. "I, sir," he said. "Why I have been through that spring five or six times during those three days, sometimes twice a day."

"Well, one of you must be wrong, Watts, either you or Humphries, and I will find out which it is."

"That can easily be done, sir. You will find that he has never been in that spring, watching, at all, as he says he has; neither night or day, for on Tuesday night he was in the saddle-room playing cards with the grooms and coachmen till past ten, and on Wednesday night he went to Appleshaw with Fanny and the cook, and did not get home till past ten. I can prove, too, where he has been during the three days, and that was not watching the snares, and should you enquire, sir, you will find that I have but stated the bare facts."

Then Mr. Fowle went off to the stables, and called up the grooms and coachmen. "Now I am going to ask you a question, and I will have it answered truthfully; if I find you trying to prevaricate I shall discharge you, so be careful. Was Humphries here on Tuesday night, playing cards?"

"Yes, sir," was the reply.

"Was he here three or four hours?"

"Yes, sir." Off went Mr. Fowle into the house, and sent for Fanny, and Sarah the cook. They came.

"Did Humphries go to Appleshaw with you, on Wednesday night?" he asked.

"Yes, sir." Then Mr. Fowle sought Watts, and said that he had proved the correctness of Watts' version. Thus emboldened, Watts told Mr. Fowle all that Humphries had said about putting foxes under the earth, at Chilton, when he had lived there as keeper under me, also how Humphries had endeavoured to lure him into shooting foxes. After a little further conversation with Watts, Mr. Fowle again sought Humphries.

"Now, Humphries," said he. "You say you watched those snares two days and three nights, without leaving them."

"Yes, sir," responded the truthful Humphries.

"On Tuesday night you were playing cards in the saddle-room for three or four hours, and on Wednesday night you went to Appleshaw with two of the indoor servants; so much for your watching the snares! Now, sir, listen to me (as Humphries was about to make excuses); you have told my keeper, Watts, that you put many a fox under the turf when you lived with Wilkins, at Chilton, but you prudently added that you were too good a judge to let Wilkins know. Now, you can just pack up your traps and go. I had recommended you, as keeper, for a place that will fall vacant in about three weeks' time, the salary being a pound a week, but now you may go and do the best you can for yourself, for *you* are the man who set those snares in Murrell's Wood."

So Humphries digged a pit for poor old Watts, and fell in it himself.

CHAPTER IV.

THE SLAUGHTER OF VERMIN.

FLYING vermin are the greatest pests of a keeper's life, breeding, according to nature's laws, at the same time as pheasants and partridges, and roaming afar in search of food for their young. They are indigenous, or —to speak more correctly—native to the soil, whilst pheasants have to be imported, and gradually localized; therefore, during the breeding season and rearing season, a keeper has to be continually on the alert, in the daytime, against the attacks of flying vermin.

In the Spring time, the best way of trapping hawks is to set five or six traps in the old nests of crows or magpies, or in squirrels' drails or nests. The best time to set them is in April, or the beginning of May. Another method is to set a pole, the shape of a short scaffold pole, in the rides of a wood, placing a trap on the top; should the top of the pole be too small to support a trap, nail a piece of board on the top of the pole, and set your trap on the board. In young plantations longer poles will be necessary, but you set your traps in the same way.

Yet another plan is to make a kind of baby's cradle near a tree. Drive two stakes into the ground, about three feet from the tree, letting about four feet remain above the surface, then lay two other stakes across the top of the first two connecting them with the tree, horizontally. The two vertical stakes should be about a foot apart. Make a kind of flooring, with lathes or interwoven boughs, on the horizontal stakes, place a thrush or blackbird's nest close up against the tree, and set a trap in front of it on the flooring. Cover up the approaches to the nest in such a manner that only one entrance is left open, and that one by way of the artificial flooring on which the trap is set. In this way you prevent trapping the pheasants, but if you put your nest and traps on the ground the pheasants are very apt to go to them, in the laying and nesting time. You may set a nest and traps, twenty yards from the wood, in a fallow field, without much fear of trapping hen pheasants.

In trapping at a pond, drive two stakes, about a foot apart, into the water, two feet from the side of the pond, and make a kind of pier from the side of the pond to the two upright stakes by means of two horizontal stakes, covered over with turf and lathes. A quiet pond in a wood, remote from all noise of men, is always a favorite drinking place for vermin, and, consequently, a good place to set two or three traps on piers, as I have described.

A dead cat, laid on the fallow field, is a good bait for flying vermin, or a hedgehog, cut open and laid belly upwards. A good plan to catch hawks is to seal the four feet of a dead mouse down to the plate of a trap, thus making the mouse look as if it were alive, and place trap and mouse in the meadow.

I will next speak of decoying vermin in order to shoot them. Take a dead cat, and put it into a magpie's nest when the bird is sitting, then make an arbour, close by, to hide yourself in, which you will have plenty of time to do before the bird comes back to her nest to sit. When she returns she spies her enemy the cat, coiled up in her nest fast asleep, as she supposes, and she immediately begins to call out and abuse the cat. She makes such a noise that she soon brings up other flying vermin from the adjoining woods. Don't shoot the mother magpie at first; let her have plenty of time to abuse the cat, and swear at it for being in her nest, thus attracting all her neighbours. These latter, on seeing what's up, perch themselves over the nest and join in a chorus screaming out to awaken the cat and make her quit. Now's your time, when you see a good chance to kill four or five birds together, let fly into the middle of the lot. Down they come at the foot of the tree, and now don't show yourself, but slip another charge into the gun, for the rest will not leave if they don't see you. Very soon they will come and have another try to wake up the cat, and so you get another shot, and kill two or three more. In shooting them you are safe to shoot the mother magpie, for she is sure to be prominent in the company.

If you cannot climb up to the nest, tie the cat to a pole, so as to look as if she were crawling up, climb up the tree as high as you can, and tie the pole to the highest branch you can reach. When the magpie comes to her nest she will see the cat climbing the tree, as she thinks, and the same proceedings will ensue as in the case of the cat coiled up in the nest. A crow's or jay's nest answers the purpose equally well.

When decoying with a live cat it is necessary to choose special localities; the best place is a gravel or chalk pit, with trees in it for the flying vermin to alight on. Peg a live cat down just outside the pit, giving her a play of about twelve yards of light cord, as, for instance, a ferret line. Lay a dead rook two feet beyond the cat's reach, or you may let the cat have it, to play with or eat; this will attract the rooks. The first one that sees the cat will fly round, "querk quarking" until another one is attracted by the noise, when this other one will do the same, and so on until there will be fifty or a hundred rooks, all flying round and grumbling at the cat. Then some carrion crows will arrive, to find out what the bother is. Don't shoot the first carrion crow, because, if let alone, he will go back into the woods and tell all his friends and neighbours what he has seen, inviting them to return with him and test the truth of his story. This they will do, and, when they have gathered in force, let fly and bring them down. A ferret is almost better than a cat for this purpose, and is easier to carry about.

In trapping vermin particular attention should be paid to the striking of the trap, which ought to strike high, and strike quickly.

When trapping flying vermin, especially egg-suckers in the open, a great many precautions are necessary. Take a hen's egg and seal it to the plate of a trap, set the trap in the open fields, covering it up so that only the egg itself is visible. Keep your traps well oiled, so that they play quickly and easily, the least tap of the bird's beak springing the trap, and causing it to catch the bird by the neck. If the trap springs slow and strikes low it will probably only chop off the beak of the bird, so you will find the beak in the trap and the bird gone, the latter afterwards living in constant pain and misery all through your carelessness or ignorance. If you want to be a good and humane trapper—and it is only fair to presume that you do—see that the traps are well oiled and catch high.

Some masters will not allow traps to be set in the open; Mr. Fowle would only permit a few to be so set, and those few had to be placed in boxes or special drains, as he was very much afraid that his foxes might put their feet into the wrong place. Mr. Fowle used to pay me fourpence a head for all the vermin I killed, but, as I had very few traps, I devised a method of snaring, of which he approved after inspecting it, being assured that it would not catch foxes. My snaring-box (for it was more box than trap) consisted of a wooden box or trunk, two feet long, and two and a half inches wide, open at each end so as to receive two snares. Having put an ordinary snare in at each end, I hung up the box off the ground by means of a bow stick bent half double like a fishing rod.

I have caught a great quantity of vermin by snares in a magpie's nest. The magpie builds its nest with a hole in the side of it, something like a barrel-down tit's or wren's nest. Set a horse hair snare in this hole, and put five or six eggs in the nest; the magpies, jays, and crows, will then go to suck the eggs and so get caught. Instead of horse hair you may use a brass or copper wire snare, but in this case you must smoke the wire to take off the brightness of it.

For ground vermin, such as stoats and

weasels, artificial runs are very deadly; they should be both trapped and snared. Small, covered ways in a wood, either placed under the rides or by gates leading out of the wood, are favorite dodges with keepers. The best plan is to make an artificial hedge, five or six yards long, across any corner of a wood, stretching from one real hedge to another. Make a hole, about two and a half inches wide, through the middle of the artificial hedge, and either snare or trap it. The running vermin will be sure to make for this hole through the hedge and so get caught.

Another plan to catch flying vermin is to hang a net across a ride, both ends being very loosely fastened. The net must be made of fine glover's thread, or silk, and be about four feet deep; set it two feet from the ground, and so lightly that, when the bird flies against it, it becomes immediately loosened, and the bird carries it along two or three yards up the ride, and becomes doubled up in the net. Hawks always fly up the rides of a wood, especially sparrow hawks, which are the worst of the smaller kinds of hawk. You will catch more sparrow hawks in these nets than in any other way, except at the poles and nest traps. The net should be at least twenty inches off the ground so as to allow hares, pheasants, and above all your dog, who generally accompanies you on your rounds, to pass under it.

I have written about snaring vermin chiefly for keepers having fox hunting masters, who will not allow them to set traps in the open; such keepers must kill their vermin as best they can, the same as I had to do when I lived with a real fox rearer in Wiltshire.

I have always looked upon gin-traps as cruel things, and it is a pity their use is not prohibited, but if they must be used they should be placed under a cover, for the small vermin, and should be kept in perfect order, springing light, sharp, and high. I have seen a ferret spring a slow trap without injuring itself, but only fancy the fearful torture a poor dumb brute endures when caught by the leg in one of those "infernal machines," lingering on perhaps for hours, through the carelessness of the keeper in not visiting his traps regularly. The gin-trap, therefore, should be set in a box, made especially for it, or in a covered run, so that the larger animals cannot enter, or, at all events, get through it. It should be kept in good working order, the spring up to its tension, and the jaws catching high. By adhering to these rules the cruelty of the traps now used will be reduced to a minimum, as they will catch to kill outright and at once, and not to maim the animal, and cause it to linger for a long time in unendurable agony.

CHAPTER V.

MORE POACHERS AND POACHING.

I SHALL now hark back again, without apology, to Stanstead.

One day I made arrangements with Joslin and Hutley, my underkeepers, together with the woodman, Mumford, to meet me at the hut in Durrell's Wood, about two o'clock in the morning, which was the time the poachers usually came to shoot my pheasants. We were on our way to this hut and had nearly reached the wood, when we heard three shots fired, and saw the fire from one of the guns. The wood is on the side of a hill, so Joslin went up towards the guns, whilst I and the other two kept guard down under the wood, spreading ourselves apart so as to partly surround it. I was close to the footpath—a right of way—and, as it led two or three different ways into the wood, we thought to catch the shooters as they came out, they being pretty sure to make for the path.

Joslin got up pretty close to where the flash of the gun had been seen, and concealed himself in a hazel stub, when he heard some one say:—"Here sits another." To which a voice replied:—"Yes, but I think we had better be off, the keepers will be here directly." Thereupon three men appeared, and advanced straight on to the stub where Joslin was lying. They stumbled over him, and he jumped up and seized one man by the collar; the other two began to run away, but the man whom Joslin held shouted:—"Don't run away and leave me, lads, there's only one of them." Then one of them came back and told Joslin to "leave go," at the same time striking him on the elbow with the butt of a gun. Joslin did as he was bid, but shouted:—" I know you, Jack." The men bolted, and Joslin called to us for help.

Mumford and Hutley ran up to Joslin, whilst I ran along the meadow to the end of the wood, where the path led three different ways, to Oakley or Ugley, Elsenham, and Tye-green. I thought to catch the men as they came out of the wood, but neither saw or heard anything at all; after waiting about fifteen or twenty minutes I called out, but for some time could get no answer. At last the others answered my hail, and when they came up I learned that they had lost the poachers. These latter had crept through a gap and gained the fields, making off towards Tye Green, pursued by Joslin and the other two, but had escaped, either by doubling down a quickset hedge, or lying up in a ditch.

Joslin told me that he knew one of them, Jack Monk. I subsequently got a warrant for Monk's arrest, and Inspector Scott, of the County Constabulary, asked me if I would mind going with him to execute the warrant.

I said that I would, and then Scott told me that a very rum set lived where Monk hailed from, the women being worse than the men—they would take up the poker, tongs, or anything else that came handy, and fetch you down.

I would mention here that Monk and his two comrades shot six times at my false wooden pheasants, which I used to nail up to the trees in places where poachers would be likely to see them. They fired three double shots at one bird, and then climbed up the tree to see if old Satan was there, for they had shot it full in the breast, then in the right side, and then in the left, and still the bird kept sitting serenely on. Then they gave in and left, having fired off six barrels, and getting nothing for their pains, but loss of time and waste of powder and shot. Jack got something, however, in the shape of six months in Chelmsford gaol.

Inspector Scott—he was only a constable then, not being created an inspector until afterwards—said that, as the people we were going to encounter were such a rough lot, he should call up the Henham police officer to accompany us. Henham was about two miles away, and when we got there the policeman said that he had just laid down, having had no sleep for a long time; and he made a lot of other excuses, saying that it was out of his beat, and so on. I lost my patience and cried out:—"Come on, Scott, and let the man stop at home, he will be no use to us if he does come, I can see plainly enough; for my part I would rather go without such a man."

So off Scott and I went.

We had gone two miles out of our way to get this policeman, which made us rather late, so we only arrived at Monk's house in the nick of time. The door was open, and there was a light on the table, whilst Jack was cutting his day's food and putting it into a bag. As we entered one poor little lad came down stairs, and said:—"Give us a bit of bread, daddy." Monk gave him a piece.

"What's the matter with the little chap?" I asked of Monk.

MORE POACHERS AND POACHING. 341

"He's had the rheumatic fever bad," he replied.

"Here, my boy," said I. "Here's sixpence for you," at the same time giving him the money.

We took Monk to my house, a distance of three miles. My wife was up and about, although it was still early. "Put the pan on the fire, wife, for us three," said I.

"What? for this man, too?" said she, pointing to the poacher.

"Yes," said I.

"No, indeed I will not," said she, warmly. "For if he had kept from shooting your pheasants, he would not have been here now."

"Well, if you won't, I will," says I, and on the pan went with some of my home-killed bacon in it, and some eggs. When it was cooked we three men sat down to breakfast together, and had a good snap; after which Scott and I marched our man down to Newport, a distance of eight miles, and took him before the magistrates.

He was committed for trial, and, as we were leaving the court, I said to him:—"Tell your sister here (she had come down from Broxtead to hear how he got on) to ask your wife to send over to my house on Friday or Saturday morning, and I'll give her a couple of rabbits to make the children a rabbit pie for Sunday's dinner."

So Monk called out to his sister:—"Tell Nance to send over to the keeper's, Friday or Saturday morning, and she'll get a couple of rabbits."

"I daresay she would," said his sister, grinning at me. "With a hook, too, I suppose."

"At any rate," said Monk, "You tell Nance to send over one of the children with a basket; he'll give her the rabbits right enough." And then Scott and Mr. Clarke, the superintendent at Newport, joined in and assured her that I should be as good as my word. So one of the children came for the rabbits, and got them, and more, too, afterwards.

Monk got six months in Chelmsford gaol, and, the day after he was let out, he came over to my house to see me, and have a chat. We talked over things a bit, especially about shooting at the wooden pheasants; and it appeared that he climbed up the tree because he thought the birds had got lodged up in the branches, so that they could not fall down. We cracked a joke over it, and Monk confessed that I had got the best of him right through.

"Wilkins," said Monk, at last. "I want to borrow a bushel, or a bushel and a half of small potatoes to plant my garden. Through me being in prison this winter my wife has been obliged to cook every potato I had by me, and I havn't one left, large or small."

"Here you are, my boy," said I. "Here are two bushels of sets, just the things for planting; you can have them, and welcome."

I thought he would have jumped out of his smock when I said this; he took the potatoes gratefully. "You have been the best friend I ever met, keeper," said he. "You behaved kindly to me at your house, and to my boy before that, to my wife and kids whilst I was in prison, and now again to me after I am out.

I will never be any more trouble to you. Money I can't give you, for I have none, but I can do you as much good as money, or more, for I will stop my party coming to kill your game."

It is now more than thirty years ago since this occurred, and I never had any reason to believe that he broke his word; on the contrary, I had many proofs that he kept his promise faithfully.

CHAPTER VI.

MONK'S CONVERSION.

A FEW months after Monk's promise to me I was standing by my house, talking to my master, Mr. Fuller-Maitland, when he looked up and said:—"Halloa, Wilkins, who comes here? The Lord Mayor? He seems to walk as if all Essex belonged to him. Do you know the man?"

"Yes, sir," said I. "It's Monk, who shot at my wooden pheasants."

"He's coming to you, Wilkins, let him be whom he may."

Monk came up to within about twenty

yards of us, and then said:—"Is this the way to Stanstead, please, I've got lost?"

"Yes," said I. "You know Durrell's, there," pointing to the wood behind me. "But come here a minute, Monk."

He recognized me and came up. "This is Mr. Maitland, my master," said I. "If you want to speak to me Mr. Maitland will be gone in a few minutes, and then I'll hear you."

"Did you want Wilkins, Monk?" interposed Mr. Maitland.

"Yes, sir, just a few words."

"I hope you will not come to be any more trouble to Wilkins," said Mr. Maitland.

"No, that I never will, sir," replied Monk. "I'll never shoot any more of his pheasants."

"What!" said Mr. Maitland, laughing. "Did Wilkins' sham pheasants give you a sickener the first time." At this we all three, master, keeper, and poacher, laughed heartily. It is by no means a bad plan to laugh heartily at the jokes of your employers, it gives them a high opinion of your intelligence.

"Good morning, Monk," said Mr. Maitland,

at the same time giving him half-a-crown. "Just keep yourself straight, and Wilkins will give you a rabbit now and then, and I'll give you five shillings for a Christmas box, when the time comes round."

"Good morning, sir, and thank you kindly," said Monk, touching his cap as the Squire turned on his heel and left us.

Now Monk was a very determined man, and had been a most resolute poacher, and recognized as a leader for several villages round about, so the reader will understand that I wished to temporize with him. I would sooner have made sure of him than a dozen of the others; it was not a question of fear on my part, only a bit of generalship, or rather "keepership." I invariably treated all poachers with tact and kindness, and always found it pay best in the long run.

"What can I do for you, Monk?" I asked, when we were left alone together.

"Well, said he," "I am going into the hay country, and I want a new scythe and a few shillings to take with me to get grub with, so I came to ask you if you'd be good enough to lend me a sovereign, which I will re-pay you the day after I come out of the grass country, Can you do it?"

"Yes, Monk, I can, and what's more, I will," said I, pulling the coin out of my pocket. "There it is."

"Thank you, keeper, it will do me a world of good if we have a fine hay time."

"Well, come in, old chap, and have a snack before you go," said I. And so he did.

After hay harvest Monk called, according to his word, and paid me as honourably as if he was Lord Mayor. Then Christmas came around, and he called for his rabbits, and the five bob the squire had promised him. He got them.

"Thank you, keeper," said he. "I s'pose you havn't such a thing as a pair of old leggings you don't want."

"Why, yes," said I. "I'll just tell the wife to look out some things, and make you up a bundle. Now come in and have a snack." He did, and, after a good square meal, we drew up before the fire to have a pipe and something hot to drink, it being Christmas Eve. "What would you like, Monk; brandy, whiskey, or home-made wine?

"Anything you like, keeper, I ain't particular."

So we had a comfortable pipe and glass together, and fell to yarning about old times, warming towards each other as Christmas morn approached.

"Wife," said I. "Look out some old gaiters, will you?"

She went off, and presently she called out:— "I'll bring your old breeches, you'll never wear them again, and here's two pair of old shoes that are only lying about in the way, and there's that old coat of yours—if you don't give it away I'll burn it."

"Oh, don't do that, missus," cried Monk. "It will be just the thing for me to go to work in, please don't burn it." So the old jacket was laid out on the floor and packed full of old gaiters, shoes, breeches, rabbits, and so on. Then, with this goodly bundle, and five shillings in his pocket, Jack went off on Christmas morning just after the clock struck twelve.

"Good-bye, keeper, and the Lord bless you."

"Good night, Monk, old boy." And so, with a shake of the hand, we part.

Now, as you may imagine, we talked things over a bit with our pipe and glass, and the drink made Jack spout out freely about his night shooting, his gate nettings, snaring, and so forth. I learned a thing or two about poachers from him, you bet. On the whole I considered Monk the cadger a preferable person to Monk the poacher.

CHAPTER VII.

ENCORE MONK.

ONE Sunday morning I was just dressing to go to chapel, when Jack Monk rushed up, all out of breath, "Are you going to chapel, Wilkins?"

"Yes," said I.

"Then you musn't; five Debden chaps are coming to your wood, Durrell's, to snare for live pheasants, so you bolt off down there at once, old boy, or else they'll get there before you. Keep dark, you know; don't let on."

"All right, Jack."

"I'm off by another way, so as not to be seen."

Off he goes, and off I go, straight through Durrell's wood to the end where I expected they would come in, as the footpath (a right of way) from Debden ran close to the corner. I found Shepherd Wiffin close by, with his sheep, and also five men, who had apparently just left the footpath, and were making for the wood. On seeing me and the shepherd they legged it back to the path, and made off, and that was the last I saw of them. So Monk did me good service that time.

On the night of the thirtieth of April, I heard a tap at the door; I opened it, and saw a man beckoning me to come out.

"Is that you, Monk?" I shouted.

"Yes," was the reply. "Is there anyone about, in the house, or anywhere."

"No, not that I know of."

"Well, to-morrow is the first of May (Stanstead Fair), and there are nine or ten of our chaps coming to give you a dressing. Before I tell you any more, though, I want you to promise me that you won't catch them, as two of my sons will be there, and two of my brother George's sons, also two or three of my nephew's sons. Now I don't want my sons, or my brother's sons caught, and I don't want you to lose your pheasant's eggs; you see, Wilkins, nine or ten chaps would very soon clear a covert or two. Now will you promise me that you won't catch them, if I tell you where they are coming in?"

"I won't catch them, Monk; I'll only prevent them from coming."

"Well, then, they will be there as soon as it's light, and you must get your two woodmen to be at one place, whilst you and your underkeeper are at the other place (mentioning both localities), as they will come in by the Burn water brook, down from Livermore's farm, to the long plantation at Elsenham. Have two men at each place before it is light, and show yourselves before they get on your land; d'ye twig, Wilkins?"

"All right, Jack; I'll do as you say." And so I did, and drove one lot of the poachers two miles, by running them into Pryor's Wood, towards Dunmow. My underkeeper, not being in "the know," could never understand how it was that I didn't run as fast that morning as on other occasions. I did not say anything to anyone, but I placed the two woodmen so that the poachers would see them before entering the long plantation, for I knew very well that, if five or six poachers showed themselves, the woodmen would do the same to save getting a crack on the head. Whether the woodmen did see anyone or not, I don't know, but they declared that they never saw anything that looked like poachers.

On two occasions Monk took away dogs from his sons and nephews, one of them being a good lurcher dog, and the other a cross-bred dog, trained for gate netting. These animals he brought to me to shoot, and shoot them I did, in his presence. This may appear cruel and unnecessary, but it is the only thing to be done; a dog trained for poaching is incurable, and will always be a poacher. If you want to save your game, and prevent a poaching dog coming on your land to hunt, you *must* shoot him.

Monk used to come and visit me two or three times a year; he would arrive early on Sunday morning, have breakfast, go to chapel with me after breakfast, come back and have some dinner, after dinner a pipe, put a rabbit in each pocket, and so off to home at Broxtead. Whenever he was hard up I would lend him money, and he always paid me back as if he had been the clergyman of the parish. At the time I write this he is still living at Broxtead.

I have chosen Monk's case as a typical one of the way in which I always treated poachers, and you will gather from it that a great deal depends upon a keeper's manner towards those gentry. Now I don't suppose that any keeper in the three kingdoms has had more experience than I have in the handling of poachers. I write the next chapter in the hope that all keepers will take my advice, and profit by it.

CHAPTER VIII.

POACHING AGAIN.

WHERE keeper and poacher are brought face to face, it is always the former's best plan to treat the latter with civility, old Dick's great desideratum. Treat poachers as you would like to be treated yourself, if you happened to be in their position, whether you catch them pheasant shooting at night, or gate-netting by day, or poaching in any other way. Treat them as if they were men, and not wild beasts, for as you treat them so they will treat you, to a great extent.

If you hear them in the wood at night shooting, don't hide up behind a tree that you know they will pass by, with your stick raised like a man with his bat at the wickets waiting for the ball, and then as he passes knock him down before he sees you or you have spoken to him.

"Why," you say. "Keepers don't do that, Wilkins." Granted, keepers do not, but some men calling themselves keepers have done it to my own knowledge, and done worse than that. I have been in Court before now, and heard them give evidence; instead of saying that they had lain in wait behind a tree, as I have stated above, the keeper would say that when they met the poacher he held up the butt of his gun to strike the witness. Seeing that violence was intended, the latter then raised his staff, warded off the blow aimed at him, and felled the poacher to the ground. All this was a tissue of lies.

Now, keeper, would you care to be treated like that? No, you would not, it would inflame your blood against that man, if you stood and heard him swear to a similar lie against you. Remember, therefore, that a poacher has feelings the same as you have, and remember, above all, that a time is coming when you will be called upon to render up your account to God, for calling Him to witness a lie from your lips. Can you wonder that such a keeper gets shot, whenever the poacher gets the chance of shooting him? The only wonder is that more are not shot, and this is a very solemn thing to be considered by all keepers. I will now give you one instance that came under my immediate notice, of a keeper's harsh conduct towards poachers, and its result.

I once knew three gamekeepers who lived on the Manor adjoining where I lived, most resolute men and good keepers they were, and the head keeper was also a very fast runner. These three were out in the woods, night watching, when they heard the report of guns; they made for the spot from whence the sound came, and happened upon some poachers. The poachers scuttled, and the keepers went after them as hard as they could pelt. The head keeper, being the fastest runner, soon caught up with the hindmost poacher, and straightway knocks him down with his life-preserver, at the same time shouting:—" Look out, one down," never stopping to pick the poacher up and secure him, he keeps on running after the others; he comes up with the second man and " downs " him in the same way. " Look out, another down." The two other keepers follow up and secure the two fallen men, whilst the head keeper pursues his way until he catches up with the last poacher, and treats him the same way as the others. This occurred fifty years ago, all three poachers being knocked down like so many rats.

One evening, shortly afterwards, this head keeper was returning home from a public house, when he met three or four men emerging from a bye lane; two of them attacked him at once, but he was a tall and powerful man, and defended himself well, so the other men joined in the fray. That keeper crawled home on his hands and knees, at four o'clock in the morning.

I went to see him whilst he was still in bed,

and asked him about the four men who had knocked him about, but he had not recognized any of them, and they have not been found out 'till this day. He partly recovered, but was never the same man afterwards; he had to have some one to go about with him always, and keep him from beer, for if he took a little beer he became just like a madman. He lost his place on this account, went into a madhouse—as they were called in those days—and died raving mad. He was as fine a man as I have ever met—tall, strong, and well-made. Thus the poachers took vengeance on him for his unfairness in knocking them down like rats.

Of course, if a poacher shows fight, you are bound to do your duty, and capture him the best way you can; but I am afraid that, in many cases, it is the keeper who first provokes the poacher to commit a breach of the peace. Go up to them civilly, as you would to any other men, not in a rough bouncing way as if you were going to drive them and all the nation before you, for that stirs up anger at once, and when anger is once aroused, bad is the result. Blows are exchanged, blood flows, and not infrequently life is lost, and all because of your overbearing words and manners. Remember that the beginning of wrath is like the letting out of water, you know not where it may end; but there is always a strong possibility of its ending in loss of life between the gamekeepers and poachers. Remember also that a soft answer turneth away wrath. You say that you don't believe in using soft words towards poachers. I tell you that after fifty-seven years' experience, I have come to the conclusion that they will answer better than harsh words. Take a leaf out of the policeman's book; you will not find him using a lot of rough language towards men who are breaking the law, and yet, when there's real work to be done, no one can do it in a more determined manner than a policeman.

Ah, yes, you say, but poachers are very rough men, you know. Granted, but how about burglars armed with revolvers; are not they quite as rough as poachers? I would as soon face a poacher as a burglar, any day of the week. I have often assisted the police to catch thieves who were making a raid on a farmer's corn at night, and afterwards marched them to the police station, often a distance of seven or eight miles. I have been with the police officer at the sheepfold, in Wiltshire, when men have come to steal the farmer's sheep, and have gone with him the next day, to assist him in searching sixteen tents belonging to a gipsy encampment. Then I had to run the gauntlet of the foulest language I ever heard, which the women used as freely as the men, as I stood by to protect the police officer whilst he searched.

I have been connected with the police ever since the year 1840. A gamekeeper is really as much an officer as a policeman; but, whereas the keeper has only to protect his master's game, the policeman, in country districts, has to protect the game and the keeper as well.

Whenever I caught any poachers at night,

I took them to my house, and asked them to sit down and make themselves as comfortable as they could, giving them a bit of supper and a pipe of tobacco, and telling them to cheer up as we would make as good a job as we could out of a bad one.

"Well, keeper," they would say. "Don't hurt us more than you can help.

"No, lads," I used to reply. "I shan't be hard on you." I invariably stuck to my word, too; no matter how much I might have been prejudiced against any man, I always aimed to give him fair play.

When poachers are brought before the Bench, and their case comes on, don't, if you are a witness, try to paint the affair as black as Satan in order to get them a long term of imprisonment; just tell the truth without any colouring, for the prisoners have their eyes and ears open, and they will twig it in a moment if you are trying to send them to the devil. You will get no credit, either way, from trying to colour your case, for the magistrates will see through you and will ease down the poacher, if they do not let him off altogether; thus, you not only lose your case, but also give the magistrates a bad impression of your veracity, whilst you gain the ill-will of the poacher, who sees that you are treating him unfairly. I have frequently heard the poacher say to the keeper:—"You tried to send me to the devil, but the magistrates saw right through you."

I have seen the policeman standing between the keeper and the poacher, when the former has been giving evidence, to prevent the prisoner from striking the witness for swearing to a lie; in some cases I have seen two or three policemen between them. You need not say all you saw and heard, if you are not questioned closely; of course, if you are asked you must answer, for you are sworn to speak the truth, the whole truth, and nothing but the truth; but remember that the man in the dock is watching you, and knows whether you are swearing to the truth or not.

Some years ago I was prosecutor in a poaching case; the man pleaded guilty, and was fined a small sum, which he paid. After the case was over the poacher and I had dinner together, and subsequently walked home together, from Saffron Walden to Stanstead, a distance of ten miles. My master had been on the bench, and he and two or three other magistrates rode past us on the road, and saw us smoking our pipes of peace as we trudged along. The next day my master comes to me.

"Well, Wilkins," said he. "So you got your man convicted yesterday."

"Yes, sir."

"But I saw you and him walking home together and smoking your pipes, as I passed by."

"Yes, sir."

"You are a wonder to the Walden Bench."

"Why so, sir?"

"You never get contradicted by your men, Mr. Birch-Wolfe and Mr. Smith told me that. All the Bench have noticed that your men generally plead guilty, and if they do not, and they are asked if they have any questions to put to you, they say:—'No, what he said is about right.' There is no necessity for a policeman to stand between you and the poacher, as is often the case. How is it there's no ill-feeling between you and the poacher, it's a puzzle to the Bench; how is it?"

"Well, you see, sir, it's because I am civil to them."

"Not very civil, according to all accounts, if they come any of their nonsense, Wilkins."

"Quite true, sir, but after I have taken the hare, or snare, or gun away from them, and shot their dog, it's all over. They see that, if they refuse to let me have anything I ask for they will very soon go heels upwards."

"Yes, yes, Wilkins, but there must be something more than that; what is it?"

"Well, sir, it is being kind to them, and not over stretching the case before the Bench."

He nodded his head, and asked me no more questions on the subject.

I once caught a farm labourer, who was not a regular poacher, snaring; he begged of me to let him off, vowing that he would never set another snare. He said that his wife was very ill, expecting an increase in family, and if she heard that he had been sent to prison it might cause her to be prematurely confined.

"Well," says I. "Don't say a word to anyone, and I will see you again about it. Don't even tell your wife, for if I hear of it from anyone I promise you that I won't forgive you."

The man could not rest easy about the matter, and soon came to me and pleaded hard with me, but I would not make him any further promise. So I kept him in suspense for a week or ten days, at the end of which time he came again. Then I told him that I had considered his case, and, having regard to his wife, I would overlook the offence on condition that he signed the following declaration. It ran something like this:—" I was caught poaching, but, in consideration of my wife's delicate health, Wilkins let me off. If ever I am caught again, he shall have power to lay this paper before the Bench."

He signed this paper, and though it's more than twenty years ago now, I never had any reason to think that he broke his word. He is at present a drayman, and, whenever I meet him on the road, he smiles at me and waves his hand, and I smile and wave my hand to him, which is distinctly pleasing. No one ever knew that I caught him poaching.

There are many other such cases I could name, especially of secret snaring by labourers. These cases should always be dealt with firmly, but leniently I invariably made it a rule to give a very definite warning, before taking up the matter seriously, and the following account will explain exactly what I mean.

One day I found a snare set in the hedge belonging to one of the farm labourer's gardens. I collared the snare. Then I took one of the cards that the huntsman sends me periodically, warning me to stop the earths. On the blank side of this card I wrote:—" And you must stop setting snares, Parker." Then I signed my name at the bottom:—" John Wilkins, gamekeeper, Durrell's Wood, Standstead, Essex." This card I stuck on to the pegs of the snare, so, when Mr. Parker came to see what he had got, he found a red card on the peg, and the snare was gone.

This sort of thing cured the labourers of poaching just as well as a month in Chelmsford gaol, or a sovereign fine, and caused a much better feeling between us.

I came up to Mr. Parker when he was ploughing, and I said:—" I've lost a red card with my name on it, Parker; if you happen to run across it let me have it, will you?" So we would crack a joke over it, and I would quote the card:—" Please stop the earths for Wednesday." Then I would speak to him seriously. " You had better stop the hares from coming into your garden, Parker, by putting some bushes in the runs."

" I will, keeper."

I never had any more trouble with him, and, every now and again, I used to give him a rabbit.

" Here's a rabbit for you, Parker, it will do a great deal better than an old hare, which would cost you a pound or a month in gaol."

" A good deal better, keeper, and thank you kindly."

"All right, Parker my boy, but mind *that* doesn't happen again." And it didn't.

I never broke through this rule all my life, and all the men on the country side know this, they know that if I catch them a second time there is no forgiveness for them. Such firmness I recommend all keepers to use, for the men will then know that they can depend upon your word, whether it be a promise or a threat.

CHAPTER IX.

CHIEFLY CANINE.

I HAVE previously written on the subject of dogs, their rearing and training; and possibly the remarks I am about to make should have appeared in that part of my book, but I think that they are of sufficient importance to have a chapter to themselves.

All hunting and sporting dogs should be fed at night, for they cannot hunt properly on a full stomach. House dogs, on the contrary, should be fed in the morning, or early part of the day; for if you feed them at night, and keep them shut up in the house, you cannot expect them to be cleanly. If you take your house dog out all day, and it was necessary to give him something to eat in the evening, turn him out of doors for ten minutes before he goes to bed.

Many ladies' pet dogs go wrong, or get out of sorts through eating too much meat, so that I give a few hints as to the best diet to keep them in good health. Cut up some boiled greens very small, mash some potatoes, make some bread crumbs, and cut up some meat very fine and small—not fine and large. Mix well together, and pour a little rich gravy over the mixture. The vegetable is good for the blood, and, once a week, you should put a teaspoonful of sulphur or magnesia, or a little of both, into the food. If the dog refuses to take it, keep him on short commons for a day or two, and then when he is pretty hungry, mix the chemicals in some rich gravy and give it to him.

If you want to make your dog's coat like a looking glass, give him some bread and butter and treacle; wrap the treacle up between two pieces of bread and butter, and smear the butter over the outside of the bread as well as the inside. It doesn't matter how you give it to the dog so long as you get him to take it; and this method of coat cleaning is good for all dogs alike.

Dogs often suffer from various skin diseases, such as mange, eczema, canker, and so on. Now I daresay many of my readers will prick up their ears at this, so I may as well say at once that I am not going to give any recipes for the cure of the above diseases, partly because, at the time I write this, I am keeping a sort of dog college, or hospital myself. It does not do to tell too much, you know. Sixty years' experience of dogs and their various diseases is not to be lightly thrown away; possibly, on some future occasion, I shall publish my methods of curing dog diseases, with full instructions and recipes. At present I shall content myself by giving cases of the various dog diseases that have been sent to me for treatment. Usually they have been sent to me as a last resort, after having gone the round of some of the professed dog doctors of the day, and I have always returned such dogs to their owners, cured. I can cure all kinds of mange in dogs: red mange, common mange, and eczema.* I charge two shillings a week for keep, and ten shillings for the cure; the owner paying all travelling expenses. I have had four pounds for curing a deerhound; three pounds to cure a fox terrier of distemper; two pounds to cure a Scotch colley, and ten shillings to cure a dog of internal canker. This last case was a very bad one, the discharge from the ears being most copious, and the smell most awful; in fact the dog was so diseased that he almost had to be killed as a hopeless case. I cured him however, and the dog has never had it since.

If anyone doubts my statements, I can refer them to several ladies and gentlemen who will corroborate me. I can also cure external canker, outside the ear. I have, now, many dogs under treatment for worms of all kinds.

*Since this was written, Wilkins has ceased keeping a dog hospital.—EDITORS.

I have also been very successful in re-setting broken bones. I have dogs, at present in my house, belonging to rich ladies of London and elsewhere—the dogs, not the house,—and the brother of one of these ladies gave me the three pounds for curing a fox terrier of distemper. Ten shillings was my charge, but he forced the sovereigns into my waistcoat pocket, saying that he would not have lost the dog for five pounds. If you don't believe me I will give you his name and address, so that you may ask him.*

I also take all sorts of dogs to train, teaching them to be clean in the house, and obedient to their masters and mistresses. I train deer hounds, Scotch colleys, and other dogs, as companions; I can train dogs as watch dogs, either in or out of the house, and either in the yard or out of it. Ladies and gentlemen leaving town for the summer or winter season, and not caring to take their

---

*We believe, especially the forcing of the sovereigns into the waistcoat pocket; would that there were more generous minded men in the world.—EDITORS.

dogs with them, often send them to me to keep. I take puppies and teach them good manners—four-footed puppies only, the two-footed species cannot be taught—and train all kinds of dogs except pointers and setters, I do not undertake these because, having given up keepering, I have no land to hunt them on.

I have dogs from Brighton, St. Leonards-on-Sea, and all parts of the country, some to train, and some to cure of disease. Four years ago I cured a dog of eczema, and the lady to whom it belonged said it had been under the treatment of seven different persons, who had one and all failed to cure it; that dog has remained in good health from the time I turned it out cured until now.

I have had considerable experience of rabies and hydrophobia, and I know of a medicine which is a sure preventitive of this terrible disease; I put it into the dogs food, or water, twice a week. Some time ago I had a colley dog sent me to treat; he looked uncommonly like going mad, his whole system was in a nervous irritable state, he was continually frothing at the mouth, and was so shy and sullen that it was dangerous to handle him, this got all right under my treatment, after a time.

One day I found a strange dog in my enclosure, and, the moment he saw me, he fastened on my gaiter. I took him up with both hands, and threw him over the wire fencing, then I went indoors and got my gun, and poked the muzzle through the fencing. The dog immediately seized it between his teeth, so I shot him with one hand, never troubling to raise the gun to my shoulder. He was a stray dog, as mad as mad could be, and had evidently been travelling all night. I never heard anything about him from anyone, although I kept his body locked up in one of my places, and showed him to people, for a long time. No one ever claimed him, and I never found out where he came from. He looked like a dog that belonged to a travelling van, his ears stood up like a fox's ears, in colour he was black and white, pepper and salt, all mottled, something like a half bred carriage dog.

CHAPTER X.

OF RABBITS.

IF you want to improve your breed of wild rabbits in the wood, you should kill off all the wild bucks, and turn down some tame grey ones, young ones three-parts grown. The wild does will then breed rabbits of a much finer and larger kind.

If you want to obtain half-bred wild bucks you should keep two or three tame does, and let them breed from a wild buck, afterwards turning your half-bred wild bucks down in your woods. These half-bred bucks will be able to preserve themselves from foxes, dogs, and vermin, better than wholly tame wild bucks.

"Ah," you say. "What a fool Wilkins is! How is anyone to know a buck rabbit from a doe before it is killed?" Well, I tell you that I know, and I will explain how I know and how I kill them down.

I get up a tree in the middle of the wood, and send my man to the end of the wood, making him quietly drive the rabbits towards me. I do not employ a dog, but only one man, to walk across the wood towards me, or at right angles to where I am facing, tapping a stub here and there as he goes along, so as to move the rabbits. The rabbits will come under my tree, and sit up to listen for the man behind them; some will amuse themselves by washing their faces. This should be done in the month of March, when the does are in young, or have laid down their young; and you should select a place where there is a big bunch of briars for the rabbits to hide under. Now, from your position up above them in the tree, you should be able to pick out nine bucks out of every ten, if you are any keeper at all.

You see one rabbit come lumbering up, heavy with young; don't shoot it. Then you see another who has laid down young, you can easily tell this because she has cleft half the fluck off her sides in order to make her young ones a warm nest; don't shoot her. Then comes another, rusty-brown in colour, thin, not in young, and with no fluck off his sides. You can plainly see that this is a buck, for he is all of one size from head to foot; shoot him, and let him lay there until you come down from the tree. The other rabbits will not be frightened away by the report of your gun, they will merely skulk down for a minute or two, so that you can shoot five or six times from the tree, and kill five or six bucks.

When your man comes up, let him pick up the rabbits you have shot, but you keep to your tree. Then instruct him to go outside the wood to the other side, and walk up to you as before; you shift your position so as to face in the opposite direction, and so kill another half-dozen bucks. I can pick eleven bucks out of twelve in this way; the only rabbit that can deceive me being a maiden rabbit, that has not bred, or is only a few days in young—a last-year's, late-littered young doe.

Again, you can snare your rabbits if you have any snares, killing your snared wild bucks, and letting the does go. In the months of March and April, when the bucks are hunting the does, I can take twelve traps and set them; and if six rabbits are caught, five of them will be bucks. This is no idle boast of mine, as anyone who has seen my traps can testify.

Having thus killed your wild bucks, the tame ones, or rather the half-bred ones, will have a great advantage in every way; they will not be hunted to death by the wild bucks, as they certainly would have been had not the latter been killed. These tame bucks, therefore, get almost all the does in young. It is much better to turn down half-bred bucks than real home-bred ones, the former being a much better stamp of rabbit, hardier, and more able to take care of themselves. If any keeper would like to know how I manage to trap bucks only, and not does, he can communicate with me, and, for a consideration, I will instruct him in that branch of a keeper's craft.*

*The secret lies not with us.—EDITORS.

CHAPTER XI.

CHATS ABOUT PHEASANTS.

MOST keepers have what they call feeding places for their pheasants, in the woods; so have I, but I feed rather differently to most keepers. They usually have bare spots in the wood, and on these spots they throw down the corn for the pheasants to come too. I have seen these places as clean as a cottage floor, for, being so perfectly bare, the birds can see every grain, and nothing is lost.

The keeper comes whistling to the birds at these spots, at the same time strewing the corn, and up come the pheasants like a lot of servants to the hall table when the bell rings for dinner. They jump over each other's backs, and run, and fly, like dove house pigeons in a farmyard. In ten minutes it is all over, and the food and birds are all gone, just the same as in the servants' hall at a gentlemen's house, the moment the cloth is removed, all the company disperse.

There is very little to be said in favour of this method of feeding, and a great deal to be said against it. Keepers say:—"I feed my birds on certain spots, and at stated hours, so that I can count the birds and make pretty sure how many I have got in that wood." Now, supposing he misses a dozen one day, and more every day (which often happens where this method of feeding is adopted), what good is it to have an accurate knowledge of the number of birds on your various beats? The keeper knows that his birds are steadily decreasing in numbers, and yet he is pig-headed enough to continue to feed in his old-fashioned way. I know many instances where a keeper has started with a fair head of game, and, before the covers are shot over, the pheasants have dwindled down to one-half of the original number, through being poached whilst straying from the cover.

By feeding in this manner you collect a large number of birds together in one spot, the poachers go with their guns to that spot, whistle up the birds, and make off with four or five brace before the keeper can reach them. Rather unsatisfactory for the keeper, eh? This is the way in which most keepers feed their birds in the wood; and, of course they have a right to feed in their own fashion, and I have just as much right to feed in mine, so I will relate my way.

The great art of keepering is to keep your birds at home in their covers. I don't have a feeding place in one spot, but choose three or four acres of young wood, wood of one or two years' growth, that has plenty of leaves on the stubs, and in the ditches. I throw the corn amongst the leaves in the most difficult places I can find, so as to give the pheasants a job that will keep them at home in the woods all day long, busily searching the leaves and grass to find their food. Whilst they are thus engaged they cannot be rambling away on some other person's fields, hedges, woods, springs, plantations, etc., and the poacher does not get the chance of killing eight or ten birds at one shot. He can only put up one bird at a time, and that he must shoot flying, so that he will have to shoot eight or ten times to kill the same amount of birds. He will probably miss five out of ten, and then there is the chance of the keeper getting up with him, and this has a very deterrent effect on a poacher.

Under the old method of feeding, the birds have cleared up all the corn in about ten or fifteen minutes, so that there is nothing more for them to do until ten o'clock the next day, which is the usual time for feeding. The pheasants are all gone, possibly have eaten just enough to make them wish for more; and, being great wanderers, they are soon straying on someone else's land. If your neighbour is unfriendly disposed towards you he will be sure to shoot your pheasants, and many are lost in this manner. Again, straying pheasants encourage poaching in various forms. Butchers, bakers, or grocers, riding or driving out with their orders, are often tempted to poach stray birds, more especially as it can be done easily, and with scarcely any risk.

It is very plain, therefore, that, if the keeper used a little common sense, and took the trouble to keep his birds at home, the farmers and sportsmen on the neighbouring estates would not shoot them; nor would the tradesmen be tempted to drive through the roads and lanes adjoining his woods, in the hope of doing a sly poach. What can be expected of the latter? They are continually driving along these roads; and, time after time, they observe the stray pheasants, and notice how easy it would be to get them, so they borrow an old gun and take it in their carts. They let fly at a bird, and nobble it all right, and away they drive on their rounds; unless you catch them in the very act you dare not search them or their carts. This first success gives them a taste for pheasants, and, the next time they get another bird, they begin to like the fun. Now they train a dog to fetch the bird which they shoot from their carts; then they go further and get a lurcher, to course hares; and, after a while, they don't mind joining a poaching party at night—disguising themselves, they go out for the spree and sport.

I once knew a painter and glazier who, when going off to work, always took a gun in his cart, in hopes of getting a shot on the road. I also knew a publican who always took a man with him in his dog cart; this man used to hold the horse while the publican shot the game and fetched it, and the two men used to take the horse and trap round the roads and lanes, for the express purpose of getting a shot at some game.

As I have before stated, it is not for me to lay down hard and fast rules as to how keepers are to feed their pheasants, since every keeper has a right to feed in the way he thinks best, but I contend that, the more you keep your birds at home in your own woods, the less likely you are to lose them. I know that a keeper has a great many contingencies to provide for; but, at the same time, he must be guided, not only by his knowledge in a general way, but also by the particular position in which he finds himself placed. There are many localities in the United Kingdom where it may be necessary to use bare spots, as I have described, for feeding and mustering grounds; but, as regards most parts of the country, I should advise keepers to pay attention to what I have written, my remarks being the outcome of sixty years' experience.

Before putting in your nests for pheasants' eggs, you should sprinkle a little of Macdougall's or Calvert's disinfecting powder upon them, in order to destroy vermin, and keep your hens healthy. If your hen is unhealthy when sitting on the eggs, the brood she hatches will sure to be unhealthy also. I have often been asked by a keeper to come and look at his hens, who would not sit on the eggs, but stood up away from them. "Don't you know the cause of that?" I would say.

"No." "Then go home and look at your hens, and you will find that they are full of lice.'

He did so, and dressed his hens with oil to kill the lice, but all the pheasants eggs he had, numbering six hundred, were destroyed. I gave him a hundred eggs, and some keepers gave him ten, and some twenty; so between us we nearly made up his loss. Neither his master, or anyone else, knew of this, only ourselves. Whenever such a thing occurs you should disinfect your hens, and give them fresh nests, thoroughly disinfected.

When bringing up young birds you should change your ground as often as possible; if you bring them up on *this* meadow one year, don't use *that* meadow for rearing purposes the next year. Never rear your birds on the same ground for two consecutive seasons if you can help it; of course if you are short of grass land you may sometimes be obliged to, but avoid doing so if you possibly can. In the latter case you should get the sheep folded on the rearing ground during the winter, for sheep cleanse the land, and destroy the ill effects produced by birds being bred on it. If you can do this, you may breed three times running on the same ground, without doing much damage.

CHAPTER XII.

FERRETS AND RABBITS.

IF you see your ferrets with white noses and lips you may know that they are in an unhealthy state; give them a teaspoonful of sulphur in some bread and milk, or magnesia in warmed bread and milk. Also change their food; give them a dead cat to eat, nothing will make them thrive more. Many ferrets are made ill by eating dead meat, unfit for their food, such as a dead fowl or rabbit that has been shot at some time or other, and picked up dead and decomposed in the wood, or has died of some disease such as rotten liver or squashed belly. All animals that have died from disease are unfit for food for ferrets.

Ferrets soon go wrong if fed on unhealthy food for a long time; it does not matter what you give them to eat if it is only healthy food. A fowl, a cat, hedgehog, squirrel, rabbit, rat, or anything else will do, provided it is fresh and free from disease. The ferret hutch should be kept very clean, and should, on no account, be made with a wooden bottom, if it has a wooden bottom it very soon gets impregnated with the animal's excrements, and so sodden that no amount of cleaning and whitewashing will do it any good. A hutch in this state soon generates diseases, such as foot rot, distemper, and so on, and thus the keeper soon loses all his ferrets, and has no one but himself to thank for his loss. The hutch should be made with an iron-wire bottom, the wires being placed half-an-inch apart, so that the ferrets will, to a great extent, keep themselves clean.

All the hutches should be made in the same way, excepting the bedrooms, which should be close boarded for warmth, one room at each end of the hutch. A partition should be made in the middle of the hutch, so as to slide in and out; thus you can, if you want, make two hutches. If you only require one hutch you should take out the partition, but, in that case, you must be careful to block up one end by a sliding door contrivance, or a brick, or something or other of the kind, to prevent the ferrets from using both houses. Otherwise they will use one house for sleeping purposes, and will make the other filthy in a very short time. By observing these precautions you will not, or perhaps I ought to say you should not, be troubled with foot rot in your ferrets. Of course if other ferrets, suffering from foot rot, are put into the hutch, your ferrets will be sure to catch the disease, for foot rot is very infectious.

To cure foot rot you should take some train oil, sulphur, gunpowder, and gas tar, or spirits of tar, mix well together, and rub the feet and claws thoroughly with the mixture every morning. Give your ferret a little sulphur in warm milk, every morning for a few days, very likely the claws will drop off, but that will not matter much, as they will grow again when the canker in the feet is cured. Many ferrets die of foot rot, which never ought to happen if the hutch is kept properly clean and sweet, and it is almost impossible to do this if the floor is made of wood, for as soon as it is saturated by the ferrets there is no cleansing it, and all kinds of diseases attack the unfortunate animal, diseases which baffle all attempts to cure.

Ferrets that are kept for rabbiting should never be used to hunt rats, but kept for rabbits only; ratting makes them very shy to come to the hand to be caught, besides which they are likely to bite you when you put your hand in a rabbit's hole. I could pull a properly trained ferret out of the hole by his fore-foot, tail, loins, or even by his under jaw, and he would never bite me, but I never attempted to take liberties with a ratting ferret. A rabbit ferret that has been set ratting is almost sure to be badly bitten by the rats, and this makes him nervous, and vicious, and dangerous to handle. The bite of a ferret often turns into a nasty wound, especially if the animal has been fed on carrion food.

It is a good plan to muzzle ferrets when you use them in large earths, where there is very little chance of digging them out when they lay up, it also keeps the ferrets from killing the rabbits in the earth. Dead rabbits lying in a large earth do a great deal of harm, you cannot get at them without digging the earth all to pieces, and even then it would be a matter of some hours, if not days. The earth would be spoilt by over digging, and the dead rabbits, if left there, become carrion, so that the next time you run your ferrets through, they lie up alongside the dead animal, and get themselves in a filthy mess, instead of hunting the earths, thus detaining you for an hour or two, and perhaps making you waste the best part of the day.

When ferreting, keepers should especially avoid two things—leaving a dead rabbit in the earth, and disturbing the earths too much. A good ferreter is always sparing in the use of the spade, when it is used it should be used with care and judgment. I have seen good ferreters wait for a long time, until they are sure that the ferret is laid up with the rabbit, and then dig down to the exact spot, thus securing both rabbit and ferret before the latter had time to spoil the former, at the same time doing the least possible damage to the earth.

When working in small earths I seldom muzzle my ferrets, because it often happens that if a ferret, when laid up with a rabbit, has not got his mouth, just as you get up to them after digging for a long time, both rabbit and ferret bolt, and you have to do all your work over again. If your ferret had not been muzzled he would either have killed the rabbit or kept up close, and you would have caught them both.

If you want rabbits to bolt freely, when you

are using the gun, and not nets, at large earths, you must take special precautions. Go up to the earths very quietly, taking care not to tread on the earths, or shake them in any way; when you are within ten yards, throw the ferret to the hole you wish him to enter, then stand back twenty five yards from the earth, and have your gun ready.

The rabbits will come out and sit at the mouth of the hole, before making for fresh earths; shoot them but don't go to pick them up, let them remain were they were killed. If you move you are bound to shake the earths, and then good-bye to any more rabbits bolting. If, on the other hand, you remain perfectly still, you will secure most of the rabbits belonging to that earth, killing them as they appear and not attempting to pick them up until the ferret comes out. If you move up to the earths to pick up a single rabbit you will betray your presence, and the remaining rabbits, will be very chary of bolting; the ferret will probably kill one or more and then lay up, so you have to dig him out, and thus lose both time and rabbits, whilst possibly you leave a dead rabbit or two behind you when you leave that earth.

I can, as a rule, kill double the number of rabbits when I am alone, that I can when I have a party with me. I can kill, when by myself, as many rabbits in three hours as I can in six hours, when I have anybody with me. Again, I can always kill more rabbits with a gun than I can with nets, because no noise is made to disturb the rabbits, by talking or trampling over the earths, and so they bolt better. When alone, and with my gun, I can kill nineteen out of every twenty rabbits that do bolt.

In ferreting hedge-rows it is necessary to have some one with you, for in nine cases out of ten, there is a ditch to the hedge-row, so that a quick working ferret is liable to elude you if you are alone. Therefore there should be a man on each side of the hedge.

CHAPTER XIII.

DISCURSIVE AND ACADEMIC.

WHEN it is necessary to turn the rabbits out of the earths on the day before a shooting party, I generally go to work as follows. Take half a pint each of spirits of tar, paraffin oil, spirits of turpentine, and gas-tar; mix well together in a bottle. Stop up five holes out of seven, and drop the mixture down the two other holes; this will answer quite as well as if you had put some of the mixture down all the holes, and will answer the purpose of bringing fifty couple more rabbits up for the guns.

Some keepers, I know, will object to this method, as they say that they will get into trouble with their masters when the latter see so many rabbits to eat up their woods and the farmers' corn. Quite so, but it is the keeper's duty to afford his master the greatest possible amount of sport, and by following my instructions he will not only do this, but will also do good service to both his master and the farmers. I say, therefore, that if keepers object, they are not keepers for their masters but keepers for themselves. Every keeper knows that the day after a cover has been shot through and thoroughly disturbed is the very best time for finding rabbits at home in their earths, so that if he has not shown many rabbits in that cover, rabbits are not expected of him. In that case, he is either honest or dishonest; if honest, he is but a poor keeper, if dishonest, the sooner he quits keepering the better for keepers in general.

I have no wish to set myself up as a judge of other men's actions, and should these random writings of mine fall into the hands of some keepers who are apt to put the worst construction on things, I trust that they will not judge me harshly. The calling of a keeper is too onerous and honourable to be handled lightly by any man who fancies himself in that line, the strict path of duty in all services is to keep your honour intact, and in no other service are the temptations so numerous as in keepering. Little by little they can fall away, tempted here and there by surrounding circumstances, should they yield one jot to these temptations they are lost; they continually apply some salve to their consciences, in order to stifle self reproach, until the fall, slow at first, becomes terribly swift and sudden.

Look at the instances I have given of Jones and others, therefore I cannot too firmly impress all men of my own craft, and upon all who are about to follow it, that you are placed in a high position of trust, take heed that you do not betray that trust.

CHAPTER XIV.

FERRETS AND RABBITS AGAIN.

DISTEMPER is a most fatal disease to ferrets and means certain death to them. You should never keep ferrets in a dog kennel, for if your dogs get distemper the ferrets are sure to catch it, and die; if you have fifty ferrets you will lose them all. Ferrets should always be kept apart from dogs, because they are subject to all the diseases that dogs suffer from, as canker, mange, distemper, &c. If any of your dogs are suffering from distemper, the person who attends to them should not go near the ferrets. Tell off a boy, or one of your men, to attend to the ferrets, giving him strict instructions not to go near the dogs on any account. Remove the ferrets and hutch them in the woods, as far away from the dogs as possible, or you will be sure to lose them all. There is absolutely no cure for distemper in ferrets or, if there is, I should be glad to hear of it.

Young ferrets are very liable to a disease called "Sweats." To cure this you should wash them with soft soap and warm water, afterwards putting them out in the sun to roll about and dry themselves; also, every day for a short time, give them clean fresh straw in their hutch.

A ferret that hunts wildly, or is a bad one to catch or handle, should be hunted with a small piece of string round its neck. The string should be about fifteen or eighteen inches long, a large knot being tied at the end in order to prevent him from slipping through the hand. Such a small length of string will not stop the ferret from hunting, or be any hindrance to you, but you must take care not to have it any longer because, in ferreting stumps or roots of trees, the animal is likely to get hung up round some projecting stump or root if any length should be trailing behind him, and it is then very difficult to discover his exact whereabouts. In large earths, overgrown with roots of trees, this is by no means an easy matter. When ferreting with a line you have, of course, only to follow up the line but in all cases you should disturb the earths' as little as possible.

A keeper once told me that he saw a ferret fasten on to a man's hand; he and others tried all they knew to choke the animal off, but in vain. At last the man, who was an underkeeper, had to hold out his hand as far as he could, with the ferret dangling at the end, and then the keeper simply shot it off his hand.

"What!" said I. You couldn't make the ferret let go? If I had been there I would have made him let go much quicker than he laid hold."

"All right, Wilkins," he replied. "I'll bring you a ferret you won't choke off in a hurry."

He brought his ferret, and put it on to a rabbit. "Now," said he. "You won't choke *him* off, I know."

"I'll bet you a pound of that," said I. "And my head, and a big bit of my neck, into the bargain."

"Well, let's see you for satisfaction's sake," he replied, drawing in his horns somewhat.

So I showed them, and they were all quite satisfied with the result. The ferret had fast hold of the rabbit, so I took them both up in my hands, and, seizing the ferret's foot in my mouth, bit it sharply. In a moment the ferret let go, dropping the rabbit at once, and squalling loudly. This may appear to some to be a ticklish process, but if it is done without fear, and not in a half-hearted way, the ferret will not bite you; bite quickly and sharply, and no ferret can stand it. If anyone doubts my veracity I am ready to accept a challenge, that I will make any ferret loose his hold in a twinkling, thus effectually demonstrating whether I lie or not.

No ferret will live for more than two years unless you let him have a mate, he may run into the third year but will die soon afterwards. The same rule applies to the female ferret, who will probably die the very first time you stop her from going to the male, nothing is more fatal to ferrets than to stop their breeding.

I will now say a few words about trapping rabbits in large earths. Put a little spirits of tar on your ferret's feet and tail, and then send your lad on with him. Use a line, and run the ferret through the various holes, pulling him up as soon as he reaches the end of the tether, and keeping him constantly on the move, for the great point is to scent the holes and not to bolt the rabbits. These will leave the earths very quickly on account of the scent of the tar, they won't stand about just inside the holes, sniffing, but will make right away out to avoid the smell, and then you must follow on with your traps. The traps should be well scrubbed every few weeks, and then scraped all over, afterwards being hung up in the wind to sweeten. Always keep a dozen clean traps by you, as it is of very little use to attempt to trap with dirty traps. See that your traps spring lightly and quickly, like clockwork. Wash your hands clean from all scent of blood, gunpowder, rabbits' paunches, dogs, or ferrets; clean hands make good trappers. Rub a little clean earth on your hands before you begin to set your traps; this takes off the scent of perspiration. If the traps have been oiled they should be hung up night and day in order to take off the scent of the oil. All these precautions may appear trivial, but they are most important if you wish to become a successful trapper.

In snaring the same precautions as to keeping clean hands must be observed, only more so, becanse, in trapping, the earth to some extent takes off the smell, but there is nothing of that kind in snaring.

When snaring rabbits you should take up a furrow from one end of the field to the other, and set every run that crosses the furrow, whether they be good or bad. You will find that you catch as many rabbits in the bad runs as in the good ones, for in good bright runs the hares often knock down the snares. Hares leave the cover before the rabbits, and, as they are first down the runs, they knock over the snares.

If you find a snare knocked down in what is plainly a rabbit run you may know that it is not the work of a hare, but of a cunning old buck, who jumps over the snare and knocks it over with his hind legs. In this case set two snares, three or four feet apart, in the same run; the old buck, thinking he has done you, sails gaily down the run, and jumps over the first snare right into the second one, and so gets caught.

It is quite wonderful the cunning with which rabbits baffle the snarer. I once set snares in a stubble field, by a foot path, but used to lose two or three rabbits out of the snares, every night. I watched them but no one came, and yet the rabbits got away all the same, the wires being cut in two as if with a sharp knife. One day, as I was hunting the gorse by this stubble field, I shot an old buck rabbit which had no less than nine snares round it's neck, or rather, portions of nine snares. As soon as he was caught this rabbit had cut the snares in two with his teeth, and on comparing the ends round his neck with the ends left in the stubble, I found that they exactly corresponded. So I discovered how it was that the rabbits were lost out of my snares, in the corn field adjoining White's Wood.

CHAPTER XV.

NIGHT WATCHING.

MEN who go out night watching with keepers should not only be perfectly sober when they start, but should also be prohibited from taking any beer with them. I never put much faith in the pluck of a man who was in the habit of taking overmuch beer; there are occasions when a glass of beer does a man good, but it should be taken after he has finished work. Men who come to work boozed, and keep up the booze whilst on duty, are only a nuisance to you, because, if they attempt night watching when full of beer, they are heavy and drowsy, and, directly they sit quietly down in the hut, go off to sleep.

One night I went down the wood to my men at the hut, between ten and eleven at night, and there I found an empty two-gallon jar of beer, whilst the men, five or six in number, lay about fast asleep. I struck a light and called to them, but all the answer I could get was a loud and continuous snore. Then I called, at the top of my voice, one of them by name; still no answer, but snoring. I left, and went forty yards down the ride to an alarm gun; this I sprung, and then waited for ten minutes to see if it would wake them up, but not a man showed himself. I returned to the hut, and there they all lay, as I had left them, fast asleep.

Again I called them, pulled them about by their legs, and kicked the soles of their boots, shouting :—" Did you hear them shoot ?"

" Eh ? Ah ! What ?" was the sleepy answer.

" Did you hear them shoot ?"

" Yes. No. Eh ? What ?"

" Wake up," I roared. " Come on with me."

" What's the matter ?" asked one.

"Matter enough," said I. "They have just shot close to your head, or else they've sprung the alarm gun; I saw the flash from the gun."

Out they all rolled, some going headlong to the ground, and others tripping up over the stubs. After a while I got them round a bit, and we all went up the ride in the wood.

"I can smell powder," exclaimed one.

"I smell pitch burning," said another.

"Then it's the alarm gun they have sprung," said I. "You stop here whilst I go and look. Yes, here's the case and pitch, string and paper, lying about smouldering; come and see." So they came and saw for themselves.

"Well, I never," they exclaimed. "It's a wonder none of us heard it go off. Did you hear any shots before the alarm gun, keeper?"

"No, I only heard one report, and knew it must be the alarm gun, because it went off such a bouncer."

"Ah, they must have run against the gun as soon as they entered the wood, and then bolted," said one. "This gun was set in a corner of the wood that we thought the poachers would most likely come in by."

I never told them that I let the gun off myself, but said.—"What's the use of my paying a lot of men like you to watch, when you can't hear an alarm gun go off within fifty yards?" I knew that the gun had three charges of powder in it, for I had made the alarm ball myself.

Another time I was watching with three or four of the same men, when we lay two and two, so that if the poachers ran away from me and my man, the other two would stop them, and vice versa. We were in a pit, watching for rabbits, because we expected that, when the public houses closed, some men would come to poach these rabbits.

When it was past closing time, I and my man made a move to go up into the woods, some three-quarters of a mile off; but on reaching the other two men we found that one was drunk, and so fast asleep that we could not wake him. I took a cord and tied his ankles together, tied his hands together behind his back, and attached his feet to a tree; so I left him until we came back, a period of three hours. He had however, by that time, broken loose and gone off. Now, what use to me was a man like that? Not a bit in the world, he might just as well have been at home in bed. Such are the fruits of drink!

I was out one night with Humphries, who suffered from the same complaint, when I saw a man netting in the field. Humphries was lying by my side, but I could not rouse him up anyhow, and I lost my man whilst trying ineffectually to do so.

I never took drink out with me at night; Humphries did not take it out in a bottle but in his inside, and the man in the pit did the same. I have seen the same sort of thing in my father's woods, when I was a lad out at night with his men. I always used to do night watching on a cup of tea, and invariably beat all my men at the work, for tea livens you up and keeps you awake, whilst beer deadens you and sends you to sleep. I never allowed any smoking whilst watching, and did not permit any man to light a pipe until the work was done and we started for home.

When gate netting watching I used to leave rather early, and before going away I always knocked the ashes out of my pipe on to the top of the gate, leaving the tobacco there smouldering. If any poachers came they would smell the tobacco, and suspect that I was still in the neighbourhood, watching. Often, too, in the woods, I have left two or three sticks, with coats hung over them, stuck up at the cross rides. Sometimes I have left my lanthorn burning all night with the bulls eye turned on, in the watch hut, with three or four great coats and horse rugs lying about. All these dodges are very necessary, the poacher, when he comes after your game, is very suspicious, and does not want to be caught, so that if he sees a light you may be sure that he will give it a wide berth rather than go and see if you are there,

I have known poachers come on a Christmas Eve and walk through the rides of a wood, firing several times, and knocking down five or six wooden pheasants. I always used to place these false birds in conspicuous places, where they could be easily seen from the walks in the woods, having three or four birds clustered in one tree, to entice the poacher to shoot at them in the hope of killing two or three at one shot. Sometimes a live bird gets in amongst the dummies and is killed, but this rarely happens.

Instead of taking out drink for my men I used to bring them home to my house, when we had finished work for the night, and put before them a good home baked loaf, some home cured bacon, salt beef, or any other meat I happened to have in the house, together with cheese, home made wine, coffee or cocoa. I generally took cocoa myself, except when my wife had made a basin of porridge and put it in the oven to keep warm; sometimes I swallowed a basin of thick milk.

I should strongly advise you not to take any drink out with you when night watching, and if any of your men come there boozed you may as well send them home again, for they'll be no good to you.

CHAPTER XVI.

HUMPHRIES REAPPEARS.

I PROMISED, in an earlier part of this work, to relate something more about Humphries, and although he was my brother in law I must say he was an out and out scoundrel. It was no use doing the man a good turn, he only rounded on you for it; he seemed constitutionally incapable of keeping straight.

He got a place at the Revd. England's, Ellsborough, New Aylesbury, Bucks, and he told me that he had everything on his hands there. He was gardener and bailiff rolled into one, he bought and sold the pigs and cows, brought up the calves, managed the grass and hay, brewed the beer, and in fact nothing was done without him. I cannot vouch for the truth of all this, but I do know that a good deal of it was true, for I went there and saw for myself. He told me also that his master wanted a new coach road made, and that he had the job, the agreement being that he was to put one load of gravel to the yard. Instead, he only put sixty loads to a hundred yards, dividing the profits thus illegally made between himself and the man who carted the gravel.

Then he told me that Mrs. England wanted a lawn made larger, and commissioned him to get some shrubs to plant on the lawn, and this is how he got them. One moonlight night he and his man, Jack, went to Lady Franklin's shrubberies and took away a quantity of choice evergreens. These he planted early in the morning on his master's lawn, and as soon as Mrs. England had finished breakfast he went and told her that he had procured the shrubs, and planted them on the lawn. She came out to see them, and admired them greatly.

"A very nice assortment, Humphries," said she. "Where did you get them from?"

"Mr. Lane's, at Berkhampstead," replied he, readily. How he would have got on if the lady had asked to look at the bill, I can't say.

The man, Jack, was soon afterwards sent to Aylesbury for trial, on a charge of stealing hay from the Stockyard to feed his donkey with. Why Humphries acted like that towards his accomplice in the plant theft I can't say, it seems to me that he must have forgotten the old adage that when rogues fall out the honest man gets his own; anyhow, for reasons best known to himself, Humphries sent off his old pal, Jack, to Aylesbury, to take his trial for theft.

This Jack had a daughter, who was either going to service or coming home for a holiday, I forget which; and, in order to take her and her box, he borrowed a donkey and cart from a neighbour. Now village donkeys are not over-well fed, and, before starting for the railway station, Jack was foolish enough to appropriate an armful of hay out of one of the stacks belonging to Mr. England. Humphries caught him in the act, but, as Mr. England did not want to prosecute, the grand jury threw out the bill against him. You can bet your boots however that Jack never forgave Humphries, who had not only behaved feloniously himself, but had induced others to do so as well, and then had turned round upon his former accomplice.

I suppose Humphries was one of those characters who, every now and then, are troubled with a conscience; and that, when such an untoward event did occur, he made up for any shortcomings on his own part by acting in a doubly moral capacity, for the time being, towards others. He was so sure of his situation, nothing could be done without him; he was entirely above suspicion, so he thought, but he made a slight mistake when he tried to oust Jack, and so he soon found.

Jack and the cook were on very friendly terms, whilst she and Humphries were sworn foes, and one morning as the latter came back from breakfast, he saw Jack carrying a scuttle of coals into the scullery for the cook. Thereupon he immediately accused Jack of idling away his time, and robbing his master of a full day's work, Jack having nothing to do with the coals. Humphries worked himself up into a fury, and began to shout loudly, when he found Jack treated him with contemptuous indifference. Then the cook comes up and joins in the fray, rounding sharply on Humphries. Soon the noise reaches the dining room, and out comes master, mistress, and the young ladies, to see what it was all about. Then Humphries poses as the honest steward, lodging grievous complaint against Jack for robbing his master, This drew forth a bitter retort from Jack, who said:—"If I was half as big a rogue as you, I'd take a rope and hang myself."

"What do you mean?" demanded Humphries, and then Mrs. England reproved Jack, saying:—"You ought not to speak of Humphries like that."

"I don't rob you like he does, I can tell

you, ma'am," said Jack, whereupon Humphries swore that he would make him prove his words.

"I'll do that without the making," said Jack. "You rob your master of his barley meal to fat your pigs on; you make me take home to your house a bushel of barley meal, and a bushel and a half of your master's meal from the meal that the bacon hogs are fattening on here."

On hearing this, Mrs. England began to question Humphries a little as to what barley meal he had. "Where do you get it from," said she, "the mill, I suppose?"

"Yes, ma'am," said Humphries.

"Then, of course, you have your bills?"

"Oh, yes, ma'am."

"Well, when you return from your dinner, just bring the bills for satisfaction's sake."

"Yes, ma'am, I will." When he came back from dinner, however, he brought no bills, but lots of excuses; he had mislaid or lost them, his wife had lit the fire with them, at any rate he couldn't find them.

Then Mrs. England went to the mill, and asked if Humphries had had any barley meal there.

"Oh, yes, ma'am, he has had a lot," said the miller, referring to his book. "Here's two sacks on the 1st, two on the 9th, and two on the 18th, down to you, ma'am."

"Yes, but is there any meal down to his own account?" asked Mrs. England.

The miller looked rather bewildered. "Oh, no, ma'am, he don't have any on his own account."

"Does he have any, and pay for it at the time?"

"No, ma'am, he only opened the account in your name." On hearing this, Mrs. England returned home, summoned Humphries, and took him to task. He, seeing the game was up, and, fearing that his other irregularities would soon come to light and consign him to prison, sold off his stock, made a bolt of it, and came to me at Stansted.

CHAPTER XVII.

HUMPHRIES RE-APPEARS AND DISAPPEARS.

HUMPHRIES arrived at Stansted some time after the poaching affray, in which Joslin cut such a creditable figure, happened. I don't know whether Joslin was ashamed of his cowardly behaviour, or whether he turned sulky, but, anyhow, he gave me to understand that he would do the same thing again if he came into contact with any more poachers. So Joslin was discharged, and Humphries, being at hand and in want of a place, was taken on as underkeeper.

I think I have before mentioned that

Humphries was my brother-in-law, he having married my sister. I always knew that he was a slippery card and wanted looking after well, but when I took him on at Stansted I did not know of his disgraceful conduct at Mr. England's. If I had known he certainly would not have got the post of underkeeper at Stansted. As it was, he soon commenced his artful tricks, setting every one by the ears. He never seemed so happy as when he was doing some questionable action that would most probably embroil you with your master or someone else, and never lost an opportunity of this kind, being utterly callous as to the consequences that might accrue to you. He was utterly unmindful of any favours conferred upon him, he would give you a quantity of lip gratitude at the time and there his gratitude ended; in fact, a more unprincipled blackguard could not easily be found. This character was now my underkeeper, and I soon found out that I must have my wits about me to keep up sides with him.

He boasted to my mother that he was going

to live with me at Stansted, saying that I had done well there, and he was going to see if he couldn't do as well, winding up by informing her that he would have my place before long. He tried to work me out, as he did Watts at Chute Lodge, and with the same result, for he only got himself out.

One Sunday morning, soon after he had come there, he came to my house, and said, in a bouncing way:—" Mr. Maitland looked in on me this morning on his way from church, and asked me a great many questions about you."

"Oh! did he, Mr. Humphries?" said I. "And pray what did he ask you about me?"

"He asked me if you had taken out that young dog, yet."

The next Sunday I went up near the church, and stood under a bunch of firs, where I could see all the people coming out of church. Presently I saw Mr. Humphries come out of his cottage, which was close to the church, and saunter about the corner, gazing furtively towards the church door, and being evidently on the watch for the break up of the congregation. As soon as he spied the Squire coming out, he appeared round the corner with a pitcher in his hand, and made for a well that stood a yard or two from the pathway by which the Squire and his family returned home through the park, timing himself to arrive so as to run full butt up against the Squire. He made a dead stop, and put his hand to his hat; the Squire returned the salute and passed on, so that Mr. Humphries did not get the chance of speaking to him, or saying anything he might have wished to say. After dinner he came down to my house.

"Did the Squire call on you this morning?" said I.

"Yes, he did."

"Oh! Did he ask you any more questions about me, Humphries?"

"Yes, he stopped as he passed the house, and called on me to know if you had taken out the young dogs last week.

"Indeed, now look here, Humphries, to-morrow is Lady day, the 25th of March, my settling day for the year's game account, and when I settle that I'll settle the questioning about the dogs. I don't believe the Squire has ever questioned you about my doing my duty to the dogs, as you say he has done, or has said anything at all about me to you. What's more, I just tell you that I was up among the fir trees by the Black pond, and saw you waiting for the Squire to come out of church, I saw you meet him at the well, and he passed on and never said a word to you; yet you tell me he stopped, and called you to ask about me and the young dogs. I don't believe a word you say."

Humphries saw he had made a mistake, and quickly altered his tone; he begged me not to mention the matter, and excused himself by saying that the squire had accosted him as he passed the house some time previously, and had asked him if he had heard me say how the young dog was getting on, and whether it was likely to turn out a good one or not. So there the matter ended.

But Humphries could not remain quiet for

long, he passed from one dodge to another, to try and get me out of my place; he told me to my face that I had been lord over the estate long enough, but that I was about to come off my throne.

"Well," said I, "It will take a better man than you to dethrone me."

"Will it?" says he, "We'll see all about that, Wilkins."

This was an anxious time for me, and I deeply regretted having taken him on as underkeeper; I saw that he intended to do me as much harm as he could, and, as no one but myself knew his slippery character, he could injure me in a hundred ways without drawing suspicion on himself. This man was my sister's husband! I anxiously awaited an opportunity to get rid of him, and at last it came.

One day he trapped a fox, brought it down into Durrell's Wood, and pegged it down in one of the rides. The hounds were coming that morning, but I happened to walk up the ride before they came, found the fox, and took it away. Had the hounds come across a fox in a trap it would have been useless for me to deny that I knew anything about it being there, I should have got the credit of being a fox-destroyer, and the Hunt would have thought me one, even if I cleared myself with my master.

I knew very well that Humphries had done it, and 1 accused him of it; of course he denied it on oath. As I told him, however, if he didn't put it there who did? I know fox runs, and there was no run in that place through Durrell's Wood, therefore it must have been a malicious act on the part of some one, and designed to get me into a scrape. Who was the most likely person to play me a scurvy trick? Anyhow the dodge failed, it didn't take, but he tried many other such dodges afterwards, and they all failed.

One Sunday he caught three tradesmen, so he said, trespassing after rabbits in a gorse bank. He swore before the magistrates that all three men were racing a rabbit up and down the ditch, stopping at every hole, putting their arms in, and searching every hole in the bank. Here one of the magistrates asked him if there were many rabbit-holes in that bank.

'Yes, sir," said he, "A great many."

"How long were they at the bank?"

"Ten or fifteen minutes, sir."

"And are there many large earths or, properly speaking, burrows in the bank?"

"Yes, sir, one earth reaches forty or fifty yards, and is full of holes."

"And these men stopped at every hole, and put their arms into each of them?"

"Yes, sir."

"In ten or fifteen minutes?"

"Yes, sir."

The magistrate turned to me. "Wilkins," said he, "you know this bank I suppose?"

"Yes, sir," said I.

"Well, how long would it take you to put your hand up all the rabbit burrows in that bank?"

"A good half a day, I think, sir."

"Yet, according to Humphries, these men did it in ten or fifteen minutes!" And the magistrates forthwith dismissed the case, and severely reprimanded Humphries, telling him to be careful, on all future occasions, to speak the truth in the witness box.

Now I come to one of the most curious episodes of my life, and one that played an important part in Humphries' removal, it being nothing more or less than a dream.

I write it down exactly as I dreamt it, for, although it is a long time ago, it made an impression on my mind that has never been effaced.

I dreamt that Humphries and I were coming from Bishop Stortford through Birchanger Wood, and, as soon as we got out of the wood into the footpath that ran through the field, we passed a sheep fold, the sheep in it lying alongside the hurdles close to the footpath. As we were walking along, Humphries put his hand through, or his arm over, the hurdles, seized a lamb, and tucked it away under his left arm.

"What are you going to do with that?" says I.

"Hush, hush!" says he, holding up his finger warningly, to induce me to hold my tongue.

"If a policeman met you with it he would think you meant to steal it," says I.

"Hush, hush," said he again. Then, stepping off the path on to a newly ploughed field, he walked up the furrow and, turning over a sod, stuck the lamb with his knife. He let the blood flow under the sod, and, as soon as the lamb was dead, he turned the sod back in its place again, thus covering up the blood. Then he rejoined me, carrying with him the dead lamb.

"If I am asked anything about this," says I, "I shall tell the truth, and you must take the consequences."

At this point the dream unaccountably changed. Although Humphries was still the chief actor, the circumstances were different. I never awoke during the whole time—or, if I did, I was not conscious of it—but kept dreaming right on.

I dreamt that Humphries came to me and

said: "This is a pretty job; Mr. Newman has given his men leave to snare all the hares in his standing corn on the farm. I have given him a receipt for it, though—I went and mowed down all his green oats in the honeysuckle field, to pay him out for it."

"Why," says I, "they'll get the print of your foot in the field, and find you out as sure as you stand there, Humphries. Which way did you come home from the field?"

"I crossed Bury Lodge Road into Parkfield, then up by the swede turnips and hurdles where the sheep are folded, along Burton End Road to the chaseway, and so to my house by the Hall garden."

"They will track you to your house, then?"

"No, they won't, for the sheep have gone through the chase out of Parkfield, and put the footmarks out. But, as I crossed the road out of Parkfield to the chaseway, three of Mr. Newman's men met me with my scythe on my shoulder as they were going to their work.

"Well, Humphries," says I, "those men will be sure to tell their master, when it becomes known that the oats in the honeysuckle field are cut down, that they met you carrying a scythe at the break of day."

"What can I do to prevent them finding me out, keeper?" says he.

"Do?" says I. "Do the best you can."

"Well, tell me, you can if you like."

"There," says I, "take your scythe, and go into the Round Coppice, and mow the rides as quickly as ever you can, then, if you are questioned about carrying the scythe, you can say that you were bringing it home from the wood. Also, take your shoes, tie them together, put a big stone in each one, and sink them in the Black Pond, so that they can't get the print of the nails in your shoes."

"I'll go and do as you say at once," says he. And here my dream ended.

The next morning I was telling Humphries the extraordinary dream I had had, when up comes Inspector Scott, and, seeing us together near the dog kennel, he called out to me: "Wilkins, I want you to come with me to Green End farm; bring a blood-hound or

HUMPHRIES REAPPEARS. 437

retriever with you, as I want to search for a lamb, or its skin, that was stolen last night."

"Just loose the dogs," said I, turning to Humphries, and then Scott and I started off, but found nothing. Scott thought we might find out the place where it was killed, or come across the insides and skin in some ditch, but our search proved fruitless.

Some ten days afterwards Scott came to me, and said:—"Humphries has got some roots of trees in the coppice that he wants me to buy for firewood, I am going over there to-morrow to look at them, do you mind my taking his gun and trying for a rabbit?"

"Oh, no! you may do that, and welcome," said I.

The day after that Scott came to me again, and said:—"I had a good look at those roots yesterday, and then left Humphries sitting by them whilst I went down the ride in search of a rabbit. Lo and behold! I came across the print of the boot or shoe I tracked from Green end farm to Parkfield gateway. If you remember, Wilkins, I had grave suspicions that the owner of those shoes was the lamb thief, and I told you that the shoe had very large nails in it, the largest I ever saw in my life. I also said that the wearer must have been a tall man, as I could not step in the long strides he took."

"Good gracious!" said I, a sudden thought striking me. "Those shoes belong to my man, Humphries; he had them made at Chesham when he was underkeeper for my father there. The blacksmith makes the nails specially to suit the ground, which is very stony, and puts twelve nails, each as large as a shilling piece, in one shoe, with tips besides.

"There, now," said Scott, " I counted the number of nail prints, both in the wood yesterday, and at Green end farm, and it was twelve in each case; I took the length of the shoe, and it was the same in both cases. I tracked the prints nearly all the way from his house to Green end farm; I have not the least doubt but what he stole the lamb. Shall you be at home after dinner to-morrow? if you are, I'll come up and tell you more about it;

I'm off to Henham, now, to look after some more stolen property there."

"Very well," said I, "I'll wait for you to-morrow." Next day he arrived after dinner, and we set off together to have a good look round Humphries' cottage. At the dog's kennel we saw a lamb's lower jaw bone, and the dog lying alongside a pile of mutton or lamb bones, whilst the pig-stye was strewn with small bones, and the trough was full of mutton fat. Scott and I talked the matter over, and he said that there was no chance of identifying the meat after such a long time had elapsed, and, considering that most of it appeared to be in the stomachs of the pigs and dog, I quite agreed with him. He said that Humphries might possibly be convicted by the circumstantial evidence, but it was uncertain, so, although both of us believed Humphries to be guilty, we decided to get rid of him, merely, and not to prosecute.

A few weeks after this I packed Mr. Humphries off to Australia, and very glad I was to get rid of him. Before he went, however, I related the whole story to his wife, my sister, and she said that she was sure that my suspicions were correct. "You know, John," said she, "I was ill and upstairs at the time, and the nurse brought me lamb for dinner, lamb for supper, and lamb again next day. It was nothing but lamb, lamb, lamb, 'till I sent for Edward, and asked him what all this lamb meant. I said: 'Are you feeding me on my brother John's dogs' meat? It must be some dead lamb John has got for his dogs.' But he declared to me that it was not, saying that you did not know he had bought any lamb. 'Well, Edward,' said I, 'this lamb was never killed by a butcher, or it wouldn't be hacked about so; besides, you would never buy all this quantity at one time. It must be meat you've had from John's dogs, and I won't touch any more of it.' Then he boiled it up, and fed his dog and pigs on the remainder."

My sister asked me not to say anything to Humphries, stating that, as soon as they arrived in Australia, she would talk to him about it.

I never heard any more about the subject

until a few years afterwards, when a most damning piece of evidence turned up unexpectedly. The Black Pond was being cleared out, and, as I was crossing the park, one of the men engaged on the job called me to look at a pair of shoes he had found in the mud. "Such curious shoes as I have never seen before, keeper," said he. I recognized them in a moment; they were Humphries', the ones that Inspector Scott wanted. I don't think Humphries ever returned from Australia, but whether he is alive or not I don't know. So here ends my experience of him, and here ends my book.

Good-bye.

THE END.

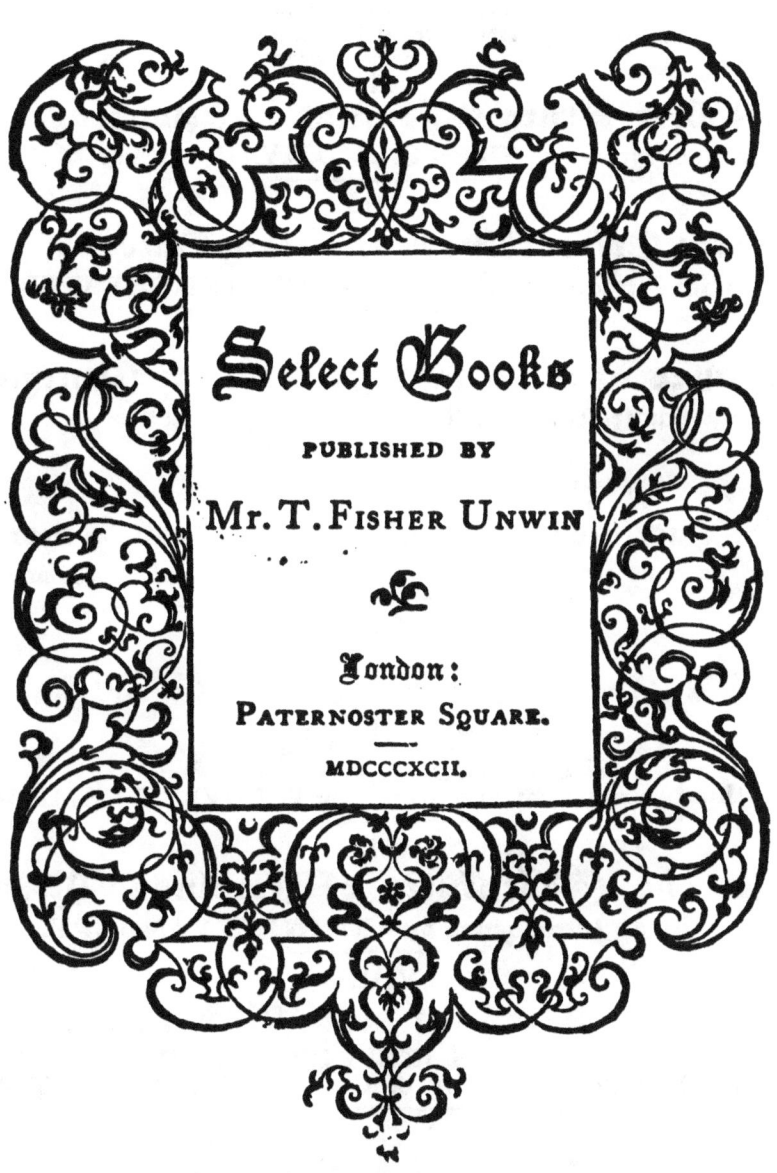

The Adventure Series.

Large crown 8vo., cloth, 5s. each, fully Illustrated.

I.
The Adventures of a Younger Son.
By E. J. TRELAWNY. With an Introduction by EDWARD GARNETT.
Illustrated with several Portraits of Trelawny.

II.
Robert Drury's Journal in Madagascar.
With Preface and Notes by CAPT. S. P. OLIVER, Author of "Madagascar."

III.
Memoirs of the Extraordinary Military Career of John Shipp.
With Introduction by H. MANNERS CHICHESTER.

IV.
The Adventures of Thomas Pellow, of Penryn, Mariner.
Written by Himself; and Edited, with an Introduction and Notes, by
DR. ROBERT BROWN.

V.
The Buccaneers and Marooners of America:
Being an account of certain notorious Freebooters of the Spanish Main.
Edited by HOWARD PYLE.

VI.
The Log of a Jack Tar; or, The Life of James Choyce, Master Mariner.
With O'Brien's Captivity in France.
Edited, with an Introduction and Notes, by V. LOVETT CAMERON, R.N.

VII.
The Voyages and Adventures of Ferdinand Mendez Pinto.
With an Introduction by ARMINIUS VAMBÉRY.

VIII.
The Story of the Filibusters.
By JAMES JEFFREY ROCHE.
To which is added The Life of COLONEL DAVID CROCKETT.

IX.
A Master Mariner:
Being the Life and Adventures of CAPT. ROBERT WILLIAM EASTWICK.
Edited by HERBERT COMPTON.

X.
Kolokotrones: Klepht and Warrior.
Translated from the Greek, and Prefaced with an Account of the Klephts, by MRS.
EDMUNDS. With Introduction by M. J. GENNADIUS, Greek Minister
Resident, London.

Catalogue of Select Books in Belles Lettres, History, Biography, Theology, Travel, Miscellaneous, and Books for Children.

Belles Lettres.

Pablo de Ségovie. By Francesco de Quevedo. Illustrated with Sixty Drawings by Daniel Vierge. With an Introduction on Vierge and his Art by Joseph Pennell, and a Critical Essay on Quevedo and his Writings by W. E. Watts. Limited Edition only. Three Guineas nett. [1892.

A French Ambassador at the Court of Charles II. (Le Comte de Cominges, 1662-1665). With many Portraits. By J. J. Jusserand. Demy 8vo., cloth gilt. [1892.

Jules Bastien Lepage and his Art. A Memoir, by André Theuriet. With which is included Bastien Lepage as Artist, by George Clausen, A.R.W.S.; An Essay on Modern Realism in Painting, by Walter Sickert, N.E.A.C.; and a Study of Marie Bashkirtseff, by Mathilde Blind. Illustrated by Reproductions of Bastien Lepage's Works. Royal 8vo., cloth, gilt tops, 10s. 6d.

The Women of the French Salons. A Series of Articles on the French Salons of the Seventeenth and Eighteenth Centuries. By Amelia G. Mason. Profusely Illustrated. Foolscap folio, cloth, 25s.

These papers treat of the literary, political, and social influence of the women in France, during the two centuries following the foundation of the salons; including pen-portraits of many noted leaders of famous coteries, and giving numerous glimpses of the Society of this brilliant period.

The Real Japan. Studies of Contemporary Japanese Manners, Morals, Administrations, and Politics. By HENRY NORMAN. Illustrated with about 50 Photographs taken by the Author. Crown 8vo., cloth, 10s. 6d.

EXTRACT FROM PREFACE.—These essays constitute an attempt, *faute de mieux*, to place before the readers of the countries whence Japan is deriving her incentives and her ideas, an account of some of the chief aspects and institutions of Japanese life as it really is to-day.

The Stream of Pleasure. A Narrative of a Journey on the Thames from Oxford to London. By JOSEPH and ELIZABETH ROBINS PENNELL. Profusely Illustrated by JOSEPH PENNELL. Small Crown 4to., cloth, 7s. 6d.

"Mrs. Pennell is bright and amusing. Mr. Pennell's sketches of river-side bits and nooks are charming; and a useful practical chapter has been written by Mr. J. G. Legge. The book is an artistic treat."—*Scotsman*.

Gypsy Sorcery and Fortune Telling. Illustrated by numerous Incantations, Specimens of Medical Magic, Anecdotes and Tales, by CHARLES GODFREY LELAND ("Hans Breitmann"). Illustrations by the Author. Small 4to., cloth, 16s. Limited Edition of 150 Copies, price £1 11s. 6d. nett.

"The student of folk-lore will welcome it as one of the most valuable additions recently made to the literature of popular beliefs."—*Scotsman*.

Esther Pentreath, the Miller's Daughter: A Cornish Romance. By J. H. PEARCE, Author of "Bernice," &c. 6s.

Mr. LEONARD COURTNEY, M.P., in the *Nineteenth Century* for May, says it is "an idyll that captivates us by its tenderness, its grace, and its beauty.... In truth, the special distinction of 'Esther Pentreath' may be said to lie in the poetic gift of its author."

Main-travelled Roads. Six Mississippi-Valley Stories. By HAMLIN GARLAND. Crown 8vo., cloth, 3s. 6d.

"Main-travelled Roads" depicts the hard life of the average American Farmer and the farm hands. The author has lived the life he tells of, and he may be called a true realist in his art.

The English Novel in the Time of Shakespeare. By J. J. JUSSERAND, Author of "English Wayfaring Life." Translated by ELIZABETH LEE, Revised and Enlarged by the Author. Illustrated. Demy 8vo., cloth, 21s.

"M. Jusserand's fascinating volume."—*Quarterly Review*.

English Wayfaring Life in the Middle Ages (XIVth Century). By J. J. JUSSERAND. Translated from the French by LUCY A. TOULMIN SMITH. Illustrated. Fourth Edition. Crown 8vo., cloth, 7s. 6d.

"This is an extremely fascinating book, and it is surprising that several years should have elapsed before it was brought out in an English dress. However, we have lost nothing by waiting."—*Times.*

Dreams. By OLIVE SCHREINER, Author of "The Story of an African Farm." With Portrait. Third Edition. Fcap. 8vo., buckram, gilt, 6s.

"They can be compared only with the painted allegories of Mr. Watts.... The book is like nothing else in English. Probably it will have no successors as it has had no forerunners."—*Athenæum.*

Gottfried Keller: A Selection of his Tales. Translated, with a Memoir, by KATE FREILIGRATH KROEKER, Translator of "Brentano's Fairy Tales." With Portrait. Crown 8vo., cloth, 6s.

"The English reader could not have a more representative collection of Keller's admirable stories."—*Saturday Review.*

The Trials of a Country Parson: Some Fugitive Papers by Rev. A. JESSOPP, D.D., Author of "Arcady," "The Coming of the Friars," &c. Crown 8vo., cloth, 7s. 6d.

"Sparkles with fresh and unforced humour, and abounds in genial commonsense."—*Scotsman.*

The Coming of the Friars, And other Mediæval Sketches. By the Rev. AUGUSTUS JESSOPP, D.D., Author of "Arcady: For Better, For Worse," &c. Third Edition. Crown 8vo., cloth, 7s. 6d.

"Always interesting and frequently fascinating."—*St. James's Gazette.*

Arcady: For Better, For Worse. By AUGUSTUS JESSOPP, D.D., Author of "One Generation of a Norfolk House." Portrait. Popular Edition. Crown 8vo., cloth, 3s. 6d.

"A volume which is, to our minds, one of the most delightful ever published in English."—*Spectator.*

Robert Browning: Personal Notes. Frontispiece. Small crown 8vo., parchment, 4s. 6d.

"Every lover of Browning will wish to possess this exquisitely-printed and as exquisitely-bound little volume."—*Yorkshire Daily Post.*

Old Chelsea. A Summer-Day's Stroll. By Dr. BENJAMIN ELLIS MARTIN. Illustrated by JOSEPH PENNELL. Third and Cheaper Edition. Square imperial 16mo., cloth, 3s. 6d.

"Dr. Martin has produced an interesting account of old Chelsea, and he has been well seconded by his coadjutor."—*Athenæum*.

Euphorion: Studies of the Antique and the Mediæval in the Renaissance. By VERNON LEE. Cheap Edition, in one volume. Demy 8vo., cloth, 7s. 6d.

"It is the fruit, as every page testifies, of singularly wide reading and independent thought, and the style combines with much picturesqueness a certain largeness of volume, that reminds us more of our earlier writers than those of our own time."
Contemporary Review.

Studies of the Eighteenth Century in Italy. By VERNON LEE. Demy 8vo., cloth, 7s. 6d.

"These studies show a wide range of knowledge of the subject, precise investigation, abundant power of illustration, and hearty enthusiasm. . . . The style of writing is cultivated, neatly adjusted, and markedly clever."—*Saturday Review*.

Belcaro: Being Essays on Sundry Æsthetical Questions. By VERNON LEE. Crown 8vo., cloth, 5s.

Juvenilia: A Second Series of Essays on Sundry Æsthetical Questions. By VERNON LEE. Two vols. Small crown 8vo., cloth, 12s.

"To discuss it properly would require more space than a single number of 'The Academy' could afford."—*Academy*.

Baldwin: Dialogues on Views and Aspirations. By VERNON LEE. Demy 8vo., cloth, 12s.

"The dialogues are written with . . . an intellectual courage which shrinks from no logical conclusion."—*Scotsman*.

Ottilie: An Eighteenth Century Idyl. By VERNON LEE. Square 8vo., cloth extra, 3s. 6d.

"A graceful little sketch. . . . Drawn with full insight into the period described."—*Spectator*.

Introductory Studies in Greek Art. Delivered in the British Museum by JANE E. HARRISON. With Illustrations. Second Edition. Square imperial 16mo., 7s. 6d.

"The best work of its kind in English."—*Oxford Magazine*.

www.ingramcontent.com/pod-product-compliance
Lightning Source LLC
Chambersburg PA
CBHW080327170426
43194CB00014B/2491